THE CLASSIC
Mercedes-Benz

THE CLASSIC
Mercedes-Benz

PHIL DRACKETT

BISON

Distributed by
Frederick Fell Publishers, Inc.
386 Park Avenue South
New York, N.Y. 10016

First published in 1983 by
Bison Books Corp.
17 Sherwood Place
Greenwich, CT 06830
U.S.A.

ISBN 0-8119-0558-6

Printed in Hong Kong

Reprinted 1984

Page 1: The three-pointed star, Mercedes calling card known throughout
the world.
Page 2 and 3: A fine example of a 1937 500K, presently in the A-C-D
Museum at Auburn, Indiana.
Below: A 1938 230 Sedan with RH drive, originally owned by the German
Consul in Dublin and now in the USA.

Contents

Above: From fragile 'horseless carriage' to Grand Prix brute force: the 1893 Benz Victoria with 5hp engine was a development of the first Benz four-wheeler in 1891 which had a 3hp engine. The later version completed a round trip of 583 miles in July, 1894, driven by Theodor von Liebig. Right: The Mercedes racer is the one Christian Lautenschlager drove to victory in 1914 with other Mercedes second and third.

A girl called Mercedes

8

It took two men and a girl to give birth to one of the world's truly great cars. The men were Gottlieb Daimler and Karl Benz, generally considered to be the founding fathers of the motor industry. The girl was one of the daughters of an Austrian financier, Emil Jellinek, and it was her name – Mercedes – which was eventually to eclipse those of Daimler and Benz in the automobile showrooms of the world.

Between the wars Mercedes were advertised as 'The car with the extra class' and for once the advertising men were not exaggerating. As far as can be ascertained, the model to which the 'extra class' label was first attached was the 1936 Drophead Sedanca 500K but the image has remained and Mercedes today have a reputation, as they had then, for first-class engineering, sound workmanship, sporting performance, top quality . . . and prestige in ownership.

In the 1980s Mercedes market a full range of sportscars, saloons, estate cars and commercial vehicles, taxis, vans and trucks. To the casual observer, the firm for many years seems to have confined itself to a couple of basic models, the very attractive and sporty-looking roadsters and the solid-looking saloons beloved by presidents and businessmen.

There is an element of truth in this for Mercedes have never followed blindly in the paths of those manufacturers who introduce model after model without ever producing a real winner. Rather Mercedes have concentrated on tried and proven automobiles. When new models have been introduced it has usually been as the result of years of research, in recent times with a heavy concentration on fuel efficiency and safety.

The Mercedes story really begins with the birth in Schorndorf in 1834 of Gottlieb Daimler, followed by the birth ten years later in the Black Forest village of Pfaffenrot of Karl Benz. No one person invented the automobile but these two Germans made it a practical proposition.

Yet Daimler was 48 years old before he got down in earnest to the work which was to make him famous. He had had a somewhat varied career as an engineer, working on guns, railroad vehicles and machinery, locomotives, tools and much else, a career which had taken him to Strasbourg, Paris, Leeds, Manchester and Coventry before returning to Germany.

In 1882, despite his age and the responsibility of a wife and five children, Daimler left his employers, took a villa in Canstatt, turned the toolshed into an office and the greenhouse and garden into a factory. A man named Wilhelm Maybach, who was to play a major role in the history of the automobile, joined forces with him.

The team concentrated on a rapid revolution engine to propel vehicles and the basic patent for the Daimler motor was granted on 16 December 1883. The text of the patent gives self-ignition as the primary feature, rapid compression of the mixture being combined with ignition by the insulated hot cylinder walls and the hot bottom of the piston. A second patent for a curve regulator to activate the valves was granted a few days later. The first engine produced gave seven to nine hundred revolutions per minute and Daimler and Maybach were highly pleased.

During the next two years, improvements were made; water-cooling replaced air-cooling and every effort was made to keep the size and weight of the engine to a minimum. In August 1885 a Daimler 1½hp motorcycle engine was patented and in November of that year, a motorcycle fitted with the engine was tested and proved satisfactory.

A bigger engine was constructed with a view to installation in a specially made coach. The motorcycle, the car and the motor bus were all on the way. . . .

Another German engineer, Benz, had been working on the

Left: Daimler's first vehicle, the 1885 motorcycle of 0.5hp, and the great man himself (above) with Karl Benz, the founding father of the motor industry.

Above left: Mercedes Jellinek, the beautiful girl immortalized by a motor car. Above right: Karl Benz, in every practical sense the world's first automobile manufacturer, producing cars in quantity for sale to the public.

Also like Daimler. Benz first produced a powered cycle but it was a failure and he abandoned it. But by 1885 his first car was ready for trial. It resembled an overgrown bathchair, having only three wheels, two large ones at the rear and a smaller, pivoted wheel in front which was operated by a tiller which steered the machine.

The engine was behind the seat (which held the driver and one passenger) and between the two rear wheels. There was one horizontal flywheel, the idea being to prevent interference with the steering when cornering.

Benz drove the vehicle for the first time in the spring of 1885. It was wheeled out of the workshops and in front of a sparse audience comprising wife Berta, sons Eugen and Richard and a handful of workmen, the proud inventor drove it around the cinder track surrounding the factory.

The selfpropelled carriage was tried out on the public roads in October of that year but broke down and had to be pushed back to the factory. A week or two later. Benz succeeded in driving half a mile at a speed of nearly 8mph. The engine was then changed for a more powerful one, wooden wheels were substituted and a second speed fitted.

To prove the worth of the new vehicle, Benz decided on a nonstop run around Mannheim, in the form of two circles. He was prudent enough to make the attempt at night when there was less chance of ridicule from his fellow townsfolk.

The smaller circle started from his workshop, went up the Waldhofstrasse to Waldhof and Kaeferthal and back to his workshop. From there the run followed the same route but this time extending as far as Sandhofen before returning home.

It was just as well that the trial took place at night. The machine covered only a few yards before breaking down. The following night Benz tried again. Once more there was

idea of a self-propelled carriage from the day he had completed his studies. Unlike Daimler, whose thoughts were mainly on engines as such irrespective of what they were used for — motorcycles, buses, airships, motorboats — Benz was primarily concerned with what would become the automobile itself.

However, like Daimler, Benz wanted to be his own boss and he set up in Mannheim as a manufacturer of gas engines. Faced with a partner who thought him mad to dabble in the idea of horseless carriages. Benz found himself a more congenial colleague, one Max Rose.

Below: An early Benz advertisement for the 'new' and 'practical' motorwagon to be driven on petroleum, benzin, naptha etc. Right: The world's first practical car, the 1886 Benz of 0.9hp.

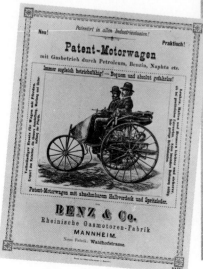

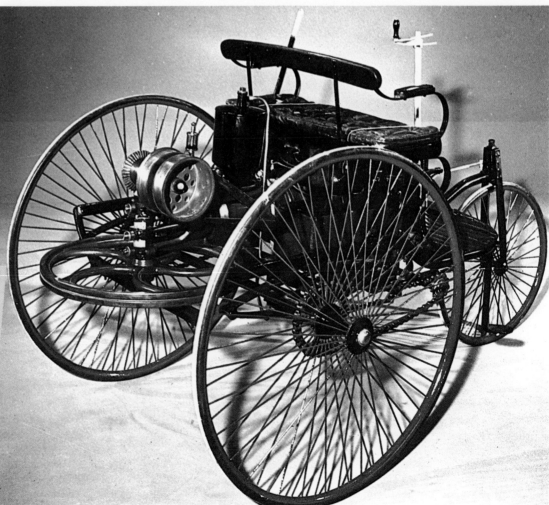

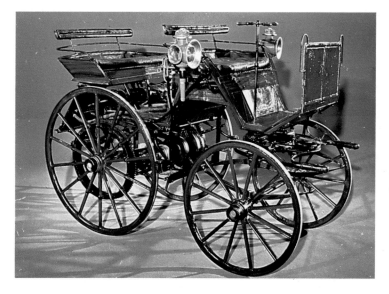
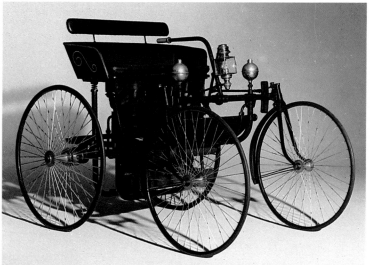

a breakdown but this time the machine had traveled a bit further before coming to rest.

Benz refused to admit defeat. Day after day he worked on the car; night after night, with a faithful friend, he would set off on that double circle which must have seemed as long as a journey around the world. Karl knew better. Each night the distance traveled grew greater, each day he eliminated another defect. The first circle was completed, the second embarked upon. Finally, he succeeded.

His friend climbed into the passenger's seat, Benz swung the flywheel, the engine broke into song. Off they went, bowling merrily along the Waldhofstrasse. Waldhof went by, then Kaeferthal. Then they were back at the workshop and off on the second and longer of the two circles. Away again down the Waldhofstrasse, every beat from the engine found an answering echo in the heart of the driver as every turn of the wheels brought them nearer their cherished goal.

Out beyond Waldhof to Sandhofen and there were still no signs of trouble. Then they were in sight of the workshop again with only a couple of hundred yards to go. Surely the machine would not let them down now? It did not. Triumphantly they came into the yard, the work of years justified at last. From the time of that journey, it can truthfully be said that the automobile age had dawned.

Weird and wonderful though the spidery Benz looked, it was yet the forerunner of most modern machines for it was watercooled, had a differential gear, electric ignition and a surface carburetor. The patent for the Benz motor carriage was issued on 29 January 1886.

Daimler and Maybach and the clever French designer-cum-racing driver, Emile Levassor, followed in the footsteps of Benz, so closely behind him, in fact, that eventually they outstripped him in developing new and better automobiles.

For the moment, Benz was the only man producing automobiles in quantity for sale to the public. At one time, the Mannheim factory was producing 12 cars per week and this in the days before mass production.

Nor did Benz confine his activities to Germany. In 1887 he sold one of his cars to Emile Roger, a jobbing engineer in Paris and early in 1888 granted Roger sole agency rights in France. An early example of this Franco-German partnership, an 1888 Roger-Benz, is in the Science Museum, London, and has several times taken part in the famous London to Brighton Run for cars manufactured prior to 1905. Even in that aged field, the veteran of 1888 has been given thirty minutes start over the rest. It came to grief one year when the over enthusiastic driver of a modern car got too close in his anxiety to inspect the veteran and an accident occurred.

Benz cars were also imported into England and some of them were marketed under other names. In 1896 a Kentish firm named Arnold produced their version of the Benz and the same year participated in the original Emancipation Day Run from London to Brighton. The car was to become a Brighton regular, mostly in the hands of the late Edward de Colver. The Arnold also has another place in motoring history because one customer, a Mr Dowsing, fitted his car with an electric selfstarter, possibly the first ever. Certainly, the electric selfstarter did not become a standard fixture until Cadillac introduced it on their cars in 1912.

In 1890 the Daimler Motoren Gesellschaft was founded and began the regular production of belt-driven cars. Although Daimler had been responsible for the high speed engine, it was his colleague, Wilhelm Maybach, who did most of the detailed design work on the first Daimler cars.

Benz by now was in full stride, making belt-driven cars which had seven or eight hand controls but only one foot pedal. Despite Benz's lead, the ensuing decade was to be an exciting one for the infant Daimler company.

Like Benz, Daimler sought sales abroad. In France he licensed Edouard Sarazin to manufacture Daimler products. Sarazin, in turn, commissioned the woodwork machinery business of René Panhard and Emile Levassor to make Daimler engines. Shortly afterward Sarazin died and his widow, to whom the Daimler licenses passed, married Levassor in 1890. In 1891 appeared the first catalog of Panhard et Levassor cars, powered by Daimler engines. They represented the ultimate in automobile design at that time with the brilliance of Daimler's engine allied to the craftsmanship and flair of Levassor.

Exports to Britain began. The Great Horseless Carriage Company was advertising the Daimler twin-cylinder 6hp wagonette as:

'admirably suited to the needs of the sportsman and lover of the countryside giving as it does full facilities for the enjoyment of fresh air and an uninterrupted view of the scenery. This NOVEL vehicle is propelled by an INTERNAL COMBUSTION ENGINE of two cylinders and six horsepower, relying on petroleum for its motive force.'

In November 1896 Britain celebrated the 'freedom' of the motorist by the first London to Brighton Run. Among the entries was a Canstatt Daimler, driven by Van Toll, with the great Gottlieb himself as one of the passengers. Freddie Simms, later to found the Royal Automobile Club and the Society of Motor Manufacturers and Traders, was the other!

Simms' friend, the Hon. Evelyn Ellis, was at the controls of

Far left: The 1886 Daimler car moved ahead of Benz in the sense of having four wheels and a 1.1hp engine. Left: 1889 saw a wire-wheel car with 1.65hp engine. Right: In 1897 came the world's first motorized taxicab with a 4hp Daimler engine. It is noticeable that the driver was still regarded as an inferior being to be perched out in the open away from his passengers.

his own Panhard-Daimler and two Daimler vans were assigned to breakdowns and luggage.

Confusion surrounded the results — one entrant was said to have put his car on a train and disembarked it at the station before Brighton — but thirteen vehicles were recorded as finishers, including a Duryea which had been brought all the way from the United States.

Daimler had reason to be pleased. A Daimler Phaeton and a Daimler Dogcart finished, plus four Panhards of Daimler parentage, one of them being the car in which Emile Levassor had distinguished himself in the Paris-Bordeaux race. It now belonged to Harry Lawson, organizer of the Run, and was driven by Otto Mayer.

The following month the British Daimler Company was floated, the initial products following the Panhard-Daimler style. In 1899 His Royal Highness the Prince of Wales, later King Edward VII, bought his first automobile, an English Daimler, having earlier had a Canstatt Daimler demonstrated to him by Ellis and Simms.

In Germany, the Daimler factory was a hive of activity. Maybach was hard at work on the two- and four-cylinder Phoenix engines which were to power Daimler cars after 1896. In 1893 he had designed the Maybach jet carburetor which was to form the basis of modern carburetor design and in 1897 the tubular radiator which was to lead to the famous Mercedes honeycomb radiator.

Even at this early stage, the Daimler Company was diversifying and in 1896/7 Daimler Motor Cab Services were

established, the company already being engaged in the manufacture of motor taxis as they are to this day.

Engines rather than automobiles had, of course, been Daimler's original aim and in 1899 the first Daimler engine was produced for the airships designed by Graf von Zeppelin.

However, cars remained the first priority and a 'baby' was produced, although at 8hp it had double the power of the 1897 Daimler Victoria, proof that manufacturers were coming to realize that there must be a closer relationship between engine and vehicle and that it was ridiculous to put a small engine in a large car. Thus the new Daimler weighed only 850kg (1875lbs) against the 1000kg (2205lbs) of the

Below: A much more business-like look about the Benz Velo of 1894, capable of 13mph (21km/h). The modern automobile was emerging from the chrysalis.

Below: The 1899 chain-driven Daimler Rennwagen was a very solid looking automobile indeed and capable of 31mph (50km/h). Above left: The 1902 15hp Benz Spider was similar in appearance although not so heavy looking as its earlier rival. Above right: A really substantial machine was the 1903 Mercedes Tourer which needed every bit of its 60hp to move such a heavy body. The pattern of Daimler-Benz automobiles was gradually establishing itself – large, comfortable and powerful.

Victoria. Contrary to general belief this was the car which first featured the honeycomb radiator although later it was to become indelibly associated with the name Mercedes.

The radiator had a fan behind it similar to the cars of today. The jet carburetor was fitted with a throttle control which regulated the amount of explosive material passing to the inlet valves, similar to the way the accelerator pedal does now. Engine speed was controlled by the magneto ignition.

It was an excellent car but it came at the wrong time. Cars were largely being purchased by wealthy people and most of them were demanding bigger machines although they certainly wanted more power in relation to weight.

Enter Emil Jellinek. Listed as 'Herr Mercedes' (Mercedes being the Christian name of his ten-year-old daughter) Jellinek drove one of the new 23hp Daimler Phoenix cars to victory in the 1899 Tour de Nice.

Ironically, the strongest opposition came from the Panhard et Levassor cars, fitted with Phoenix engines made in France under license. Despite Jellinek's dashing performances as 'Herr Mercedes,' Canstatt decided not to enter any more competition events after a Daimler works driver, Wilhelm Bauer, was killed driving one of the 23hp cars in a hill climb.

Jellinek, rather naturally, did not agree with the decision. He felt that all that was required was a car with a much lower center of gravity and a longer wheelbase, one which would hug the ground more than the present models. He found an ally in Wilhelm Maybach and when Jellinek promised to order a large quantity of the new car, it was decided to go ahead.

Jellinek had been selling Daimlers in ever increasing quantities since 1897 and now he demanded the sole rights of all sales in Austria, Hungary, France, Belgium and the United States. In these countries the cars were to be sold under the name Mercedes but elsewhere as The New Daimler.

Left: The 1902 Mercedes Simplex (Simplex was later dropped) could do 37mph (60km/h).

Maybach and Daimler's son, Paul, got to work. The new car was to have a 35hp engine of 5.9 liters, the first engine to have mechanically operated inlet valves. The chassis was long, as specified by Jellinek, and the center of gravity very low, also at the decree of 'Herr Mercedes.' Light metal alloys were used where possible so as to reduce weight. The honeycomb radiator, it was felt, completely solved the problem of engine cooling.

Other features included an elongated pressed steel frame, a selective or 'gate' shift, designed by Maybach, which operated a four gear system and had a gear lock, an original arrangement of the constructional parts and a coil spring clutch, designed by Paul Daimler. The car also had *two* footbrakes, intended to be used alternately on long hills so as to prevent overheating. Most of these features were soon copied by other manufacturers and became characteristic of cars of the time.

Racing triumphs made the Mercedes highly successful in 1901 and were eventually to lead to the name of a young girl superseding the original name of the firm and almost eclipsing the name of its founder, an early example of the possibilities of publicity and promotional expertise.

Sadly, Gottlieb Daimler died before the Mercedes made its debut. The man whose inventions were to have such a profound effect on the world had, despite his achievements, a hard life and it was perhaps reflected in the fact that when he died in 1900 he was only 66.

The Jellineks in due time changed their name to Jellinek-Mercedes. Later the Austrian Daimler Company adopted the name of Mercedes' sister for one of their models but the Maja never achieved the fame of Mercedes. With shrewd financiers, entrepreneurs like Jellinek and designers such as Maybach and Paul Daimler, the founder's death did not have the disastrous effect on the company which some might have anticipated and it continued to prosper.

The first Daimler aircraft engine, for the unsuccessful Kress Drachenflieger, was unveiled in 1901 and between 1912 and the outbreak of the Great War both Daimler and Benz produced much improved aircraft engines with lower weight per horsepower and higher performance. The expansion of the commercial side of the business was not

Below: George K. Vanderbilt, wealthy American amateur driver, sits at the wheel of his 1904 Mercedes racer whilst a mechanic makes some adjustments. One wonders how long the passenger kept his hat on when the car got going?

overlooked and in 1905 when the first German postal service was introduced, Daimler vehicles were employed.

Private cars continued to advance technically. The years 1902 to 1904 saw the introduction of water-cooled brakes on some models, water being dribbled from a small tank on to the brake drum when the pedal was depressed. This obviated the need for two brakes to be used alternately. It was in 1903 that brakes on all four wheels were made an optional extra on some Mercedes models although such braking systems did not come into use until the middle 1920s. Comfort was not neglected. Foot warmers, working off the cooling system, were a Daimler feature from quite early days.

Aside from the continued technical and commercial progress of the company, the most significant developments of the first decade of the twentieth century involved three men and their varying destinies, Daimler, Ferdinand Porsche and Wilhelm Maybach.

In 1906 Porsche became Technical Director of Austro-Daimler, which was building German Daimlers under license. He was to stay with them until 1923, becoming Managing Director in 1917. During World War 1 he turned from touring and racing cars to aero engines, artillery tractors and armored cars.

He evolved a new car, the Maja, with a four-cylinder engine and four-speed transmission. From it came the 28/32 which established Austro-Daimler as an independent force in automobile construction. The Emperor Franz Joseph rode in one and so did the Queen of Bulgaria.

Around this time, an Austro-Daimler engine was installed in a Parseval non-rigid airship. Porsche's first aircraft engine was built in 1910 but in 1912 came an air cooled 90hp engine which was the distant ancestor of today's Volkswagen

Above: 1904 32hp Mercedes touring car took on a more elongated shape than its predecessors. Mudguards and enclosed chain-drive gave added protection.

and Porsche engines. Porsche later had a stormy parting with Austro-Daimler and became more closely associated with the parent Daimler Company.

A major blow to Daimler occurred in 1907 when Wilhelm Maybach, at the age of 62, decided to leave to set up his own company. The death of Daimler and of his chairman, Max Duttenhofer, three years later, had put a man named Wilhelm Lorenz in the chairman's seat He and Maybach did not get on, Maybach feeling that he was not given enough credit for

Below: Stripped for action. Another 1904 Mercedes with strap securing hood, simple mudguards and shield over chain, and another optimistic passenger.

the tremendous success the company was enjoying. In many ways he had played a more important role in the company than Daimler himself, at least after the early days when Daimler's engines had launched the concern on the road to prosperity. Nor had Maybach reached the end of his long list of achievements. Running his own company, he became famous for aircraft engines and when peace returned his organization manufactured very elaborate and powerful luxury cars. He died in 1929, at the ripe old age of 83, one of the greatest automobile designers of all time and yet one who has possibly not had the credit due to him because he was contemporary with his great countrymen, Daimler and Benz.

Meanwhile, the first 35hp Mercedes and the types 8/11 and 12/16 were followed by a series of 18/22, 28/32, 40/45 and 60/70hp models which were known as Mercedes-Simplex. Of these, the 40hp model was outstanding. It was much lighter than the original 35hp car, partly because it had been found possible to reduce the engine weight considerably. The efficiency of the honeycomb radiator and cooling system meant also that the car need carry only seven liters of water for continuous running. The mechanically operated inlet valves and improved control of the mixture all helped in good starting, snappy getaway, silent running and elasticity. Although this design was regarded as well ahead of its time, the appendage 'Simplex' did not last long.

Propeller shaft drive was adopted on the cars in place of the chains and sprockets which had been in use up to 1908. A number of models with this type of drive were produced from 1908 onward, among them the 8/18, 10/20, 14/35, 22/40 and 28/60, all of which were in production until 1913. Chain drive soon became rare and was used only on the very large models such as the 37/90hp and the 38/80hp.

In 1909 Daimler obtained a license to manufacture and use the sleeve-valve engine invented by the American, Charles Y. Knight, an engine already adopted and proven by the British Daimler Company in Coventry. From 1910 onward, a large number of 10/30, 16/40 and 16/45 Knight-engined cars were produced and in 1916, a 16/50 was added to the range. Knight-engined cars continued to be manufactured up to 1923 and the 50hp class was especially popular.

World War 1, although horrific in terms of the carnage wrought on the soldiers of both sides, did not see the damage to factories such as occurred in World War 2 through the extensive use of airpower.

Consequently the Daimler Company continued production through these war years although naturally the emphasis switched from private cars. There was a regular output of aircraft engines, some fifty per month. It does not seem a huge figure today but in 1914 the aeroplane was still in its infancy.

The prize-winning six-cylinder 120hp Mercedes engine of 1913 was soon superseded by a 160hp engine, designed to give more speed and greater climbing ability and this became the most popular engine manufactured by Daimler during the 1914–18 period. Superchargers were added in 1915, improvements continued to be made in the 160hp engines and by the end of the war, 500hp and 600hp engines were also being produced.

From 1915 onwards, the Daimler Company began to build complete aircraft and for this purpose acquired a site at Sindelfingen. This was later to become the main center for vehicle bodywork before being used for the production of chassis and the assembly of private cars. With the Armistice most aircraft production ceased but stocks of raw materials were not wasted, being used for automobile manufacture.

Meanwhile, the Benz company, which had bought a large car works at Gaggenau in 1910, was also making aircraft engines. But, despite the war, the company continued with some car development. It had become increasingly evident that for ease of operation new means of starting the engine were required. No one seems to have persevered with the selfstarter fitted to the Arnold Benz in earlier years but in 1911 reports came from the United States that selfstarters were being used there with some success. It may be that there was more enthusiasm in the US for such things, most motorists being owner-drivers. In Europe, chauffeur-driven cars were still predominant and if the chauffeur had to sweat a bit starting the car, well, that was his bad luck.

Benz tried a type of selfstarting device in the 1913 Carpathian Trials. The possibility of electric light equipment on the cars was also looked at, an important step forwards in roadworthiness and comfort which could not fail to increase the popularity of the car. It also meant a significant expansion of the electrical equipment and accessory industries. In due course both Benz and Daimler adopted electrical equipment and electric selfstarters on their cars although at first only to order. Complete lighting equipment cost about 750 marks with an additional charge for fitting.

With the end of World War 1, the situation in Germany was such that Benz, although continuing car production, was forced to rely on a few tried and tested models. The 10/30hp four-cylinder was designed for town work and normal touring but it also came as a sports model. The 11/40 six-cylinder had a more powerful engine for heavy hill climbing work and the 16/50 six-cylinder was for long distance touring, the interior having a number of refinements designed to make a journey of any distance more comfortable.

Special features of Benz cars of the time were a chassis frame of pressed steel, semi-elliptic springs front and rear, side valves operated by pushrods, chain-driven cams and magneto shaft, Zenith carburetor with vacuum feed, electric selfstarter and lighting equipment, forced feed lubrication, oil pressure gauge on the instrument panel, oil level gauge on the lower part of the crankcase, pointed radiator, thermo-syphon cooling, cone type of clutch with leather lining and clutch stop, four forward speeds and a reverse, 'gate' type of gearshift quadrant, four wheel brakes mechanically operated, brake compensation in the transmission and a steering column with worm and nut gear.

Yet the time was approaching when Germany's two motoring giants would begin a close association which would eventually lead to a complete merger.

Below: 1910 Mercedes Phaeton was 10 years ahead of its time.
Above right: 1904 Mercedes-Simplex, ready for the Vanderbilt Cup race.
Right: The all-conquering 1914 French Grand Prix winning 4½-liter car.

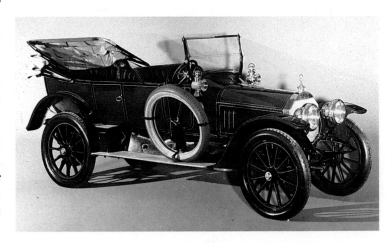

Above: The car which symbolizes Mercedes to most people, the classic SSK, 1928 version. Top: The sporty lines are still evident in the 1937 Mercedes 540k Cabriolet.

Left: 1927 'K' featured windshield sidescreens for both driving and passenger compartments and a modest luggage compartment.
Above left: John D. Chapman, of Greenwich, Connecticut, with his 'K'.
Above right: Close-up of spare wheel, showing quick release handle.

Left: The 1928 SSK, 115mph (175km/h) of speed and elegance, shown in color.
Below: Another 1928 SSK in profile.
Above: SSK again, this time without coachwork – a car which will take its place among the immortals.

But, like Gottlieb Daimler years before him, Porsche could not always see eye to eye with the accountants and other policy makers and after a major disagreement in 1928 he left Daimler-Benz to return to Austria where he joined Steyr Werke AG. It was not, however, to be the last time he would be associated with the Stuttgart concern. From 1931, Porsche was in business as an independent, one of his associates being former Mercedes racing driver, Adolf Rosenberger, a combination which was to lead to the sensational mid-engined (driver in the nose) Auto Union racing car which, with Mercedes, dominated the Grand Prix circuits in the years immediately leading up to the Second World War.

In 1934, an agreement was signed whereby Porsche produced the first three prototype Volkswagen, or People's Car. Then a batch of 30 was built by Daimler-Benz and in 1938 the foundation stone of the VW factory at Wolfsburg was laid, 300,000 workers sticking stamps on cards every week in order to become owners of these new cars.

To show there was no ill feeling over earlier disagreements, Daimler-Benz backed Porsche in building a car to attack the World Land Speed Record, the Porsche Daimler Super Automobil. The driver sat in the nose, behind him an inverted twelve-cylinder Daimler-Benz aircraft engine of 44 liters, tuned to give 3030hp. Hitler must have played his cards very close to the chest or else been taken by surprise by the British and French attitudes toward his invasion of Poland because the would-be record breaker was on the high seas en route to Salt Lake City when war broke out. The car never ran and today it sits in the Daimler-Benz Museum at Stuttgart, a monument to what might have been.

As well as building large supercharged automobiles, Daimler-Benz AG took up the development of medium sized models although the concept of medium size in those days was rather different than that of today. Immediately following the amalgamation, two six-cylinder unsupercharged cars were produced, the Stuttgart, with a 2-liter engine of 8/38hp; and the Mannheim, with a 3.1-liter engine of 12/55hp. Both could be recognized by the flat radiator and wheels with pressed steel spokes. In due course, both were fitted with more powerful engines, the Stuttgart with a 2.6-liter and the Mannheim with a 3.5. Later this became 3.7 and was supplemented by the sports model 370S.

It was the 8/38 Stuttgart which led to one of Porsche's disagreements. It had a poor reputation for starting in winter conditions. Director Kissel (the man who brought Daimler and Benz together) left eight of them out in the open one freezing night and next morning challenged Porsche to start any of them. He failed and was furious. But he soon made an alteration to the design which cured the problem.

In addition to the Stuttgart 260 and the Mannheim 350, the Nurburg, a 4.6-liter touring car, was manufactured in 1928. A six-seat, it had an eight-cylinder engine but otherwise was very similar in appearance to the Stuttgart and the Mannheim. Later in 1931 it was to be fitted with a 110hp engine and was known as the Nurburg 500. The Stuttgart, in particular, sold well and if it had not been for what the company described as the peak in high performance cars, the S, SS and SSK already mentioned, the Stuttgart and its companions might have loomed larger in motoring history.

But during 1926 the famous 24/100/140hp tourer was brought out in a shorter version as a special model with even higher performance: it was known as the K. The engine had a cylinder capacity of 6.25 liters and gave 160hp when supercharged. Its maximum speed was around 90mph and it enjoyed a reputation as the fastest touring car then in existence.

Above: The chic of the 1931 Mercedes Mannheim Type 370 contrasts sharply with (below) the more mundane and workaday 1032 Type 170H. Right: The 1936 Type 200 strikes a balance between the two. The 1936 car is very typical of its period. Motorists were beginning to treat the car as a means of transport and not merely a plaything and some of the color and glamor was lost in the process.

Next year it was succeeded by the S sports model which had a 6.8-liter engine fitted with two carburetors and an improved supercharger. The result was that it could accelerate *in top gear* from walking pace to 103mph. The many triumphs which these cars enjoyed in sporting events certainly increased the demand for them.

During 1928 and 1929 the SS and SSK added to these victories and so did the last of the line, the SSKL, a shortened version of the previous pair, when it came along in 1931.

Both the SS and SSK were fitted with six-cylinder supercharged engines of 7.1 liters, the power output with supercharger being 225hp.

Although in retrospect these attractive sportscars seemed very similar a close inspection reveals quite a lot of differences in appearance between the 1927 S and the SSKL of 1931. By the latter year, the awe inspiring external pipes leading from the hood had disappeared under cover, the radiator cap badge had moved down to the radiator itself, there were no longer continuous mudguards and running boards but separate ones and the dumb irons and lower parts of the body had been drilled to reduce weight. But the distinctive lines and promise of power remained.

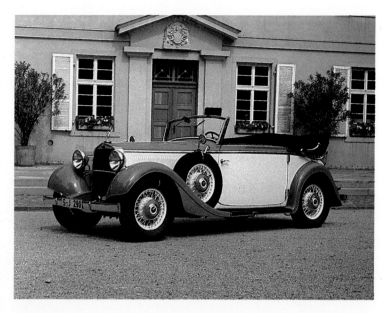

Above: A 1934 Mercedes Cabriolet Type 290, still in use in Germany, shows how distinctive two-tone coloring (which was very popular at the time) can be.

Left: Mercedes-Benz Type 500 supercharged roadster in usual form. Below: Type 500 with streamlined body — not one of the most elegant of Mercedes body designs.

Bottom: 1934 500K 'Limosine Coupe', a car believed to have been owned by champion racing driver, Rudi Caracciola, star of the Mercedes team and one of the greatest drivers of all time.

A variety of refinements and modifications were introduced in this period. In 1927, the tourers had a dual windshield with a top half which could be opened like an ordinary window. Whitewall tires were popular in the United States and if you wanted them Mercedes could supply. And at this time, of course, many models still carried the spare wheel on the running board. Modern motorists, faced with unpacking all the luggage to get at the spare wheel, may sometimes wish that it was still on the running board. Contrasting body colors became a design feature of Mercedes soon afterwards but it was not until 1933 that Daimler-Benz put on the

market the first car with a rear engine, the Mercedes 130H.

The factory had experimented with rearmounted engines as early as 1927 but the general world malaise prevented the idea being followed through until 1932 and the car finally went on the market the following year. It was a small four-seater with a 26hp 1.3-liter four-cylinder engine. It had a four-wheel hydraulic braking system and a special overdrive speed which was semiautomatic inasmuch as gears could be engaged without using the clutch.

The car was unveiled at the Berlin Motor Show of 1934 and at the same show two years later Mercedes produced the 170H, more powerful and more spacious. But the company directors were uncertain about the prospects for rear-engined cars and so they also put into production the 1.7-liter 170V with front-mounted engine and this was shown at the Vienna Car and Motor Cycle Exhibition of 1936, just a month after the 170H had been introduced. The new car was described by a reporter as 'a powerful attraction.' The chassis weight was only 1443lbs (650kg) and it had a 38hp engine. It was inexpensive (3750 marks at the time) and was a versatile utility vehicle which could be purchased as a two- or four-door saloon, a roadster, open touring car, two or four seat convertible, convertible limousine, delivery vehicle with platform or van body and an ambulance or patrol car. This proved so successful that the rear-engined cars failed to make a great impression. However, they are worth noting in the story of the automobile since they marked a definite milestone in development, as witness the Volkswagen.

The success of the 170V could hardly have been a surprise.

What was known as the 'Small Mercedes 170' was a hit from the first and its chassis design with central chassis lubrication, thermostat, four-wheel hydraulic brakes and overdrive was a landmark in Daimler-Benz history and paved the way for further models. In five years some 14,000 cars of the 170 type were sold and the 40hp six-cylinder model which was almost identical sold in even greater numbers.

Other interesting cars added to the range in the thirties included the 290, a 2.9-liter general purpose car, independently sprung, and reputedly a delightful car to handle. It had a maximum speed of 75mph. A best seller was the 230 and about 20,000 of these were produced prior to the outbreak of World War 2.

A small series of the attractive 3.8-liter 90/120hp eight-cylinder supercharged sports 380 also appeared in 1933. This model had swing axles and, for the first time, wishbone suspension for the front wheels with coil springs. Wheel location, springing and damping thus became three separate elements.

Independent wheel suspension was also used for further development of supercharged models. The 380 gave way to the classic 5-liter eight-cylinder 100/160hp 500K and this was then followed by the 540K before production of supercharged cars came to a halt at the beginning of World War 2. The descriptions of the time commented on the special qualities of these cars, which were the product of new ideas backed by long experience and which, Daimler Benz prided themselves, also made a significant contribution towards safe driving.

Below: 1936 170V showing the use of two-tone coloring. Far left: Rear view showing the spare wheel mounted at the rear instead of on the running-board. Left: The very compact engine department.

Above: A prized possession for anyone: the 1936 Mercedes-Benz 500K Sedanca with drophead body by Corsica (UK), presently on display at the A-C-D Museum, Auburn, Indiana. The car is the property of Mr. Larry Nicklin. Top left: Detail can be seen of the distinctive wheels, hinging, drophead and trim. Top right: Rear view showing wraparound bumper and luggage compartment.

In 1938, as the war clouds gathered, the company announced a redesigned Super Mercedes. The first Super, a six- or seven-seat private car, had been built in 1930. It had a 'classical' chassis with a box section frame and semi-elliptical springs. The power output of the eight-cylinder in line engine was 150bhp at 2800rpm but a supercharger could be fitted which increased the power to 200bhp.

The 1938 version included everything modern chassis design technique had to offer, such as a low-built tubular chassis frame, independent wheel suspension with coil springs, swing axles and a five-speed gearbox with synchromesh gearshift. This model was only produced with a supercharged engine developing 155/230hp. Such an exclusive — and expensive — automobile was produced only in strictly limited numbers in vivid contrast to the 170V, cheapest car in the Mercedes range, which was undoubtedly their best seller of the thirties.

With a maximum speed of more than 62mph, the 170V did more than 28/24 miles per Imperial/US gallon. The flexibly mounted four-cylinder engine was said to run as smoothly as any good six-cylinder engine. Up to the end of 1942, more than 90,000 had been sold.

There was one other development of the thirties which cannot be ignored. The company had long been interested in Diesel engines and had utilized them for powering trucks and other commercial vehicles. In the early thirties, attention was turned to the possible use of such engines in private cars and despite criticisms from outside sources, the research staff pressed ahead with their task.

In September 1933 a Diesel engine intended for use in a private car was subjected to bench tests at Unterturkheim. This 3.8-liter six-cylinder engine developed 82bhp at 2800rpm so that a high rate of revolutions per minute had already been reached, a necessity for Diesel cars. However, when the engine was mounted in a Mannheim chassis it was found there was too much vibration and this had a bad effect on the chassis.

That project was dropped but work went ahead on the development of a 2.6-liter four-cylinder Diesel engine, the cylinders of which were the same size as those of the 3.8-liter engine. The problems associated with injection pumps, nozzles and power control had been practically solved by means

Illustrated here are three variations on a theme. Left: 1936 Mercedes-Benz Cabriolet 540K (105mph, 170km/h). Above: 1938 540K Sindlefingen Cabriolet A. Below: 1939 Sindlefingen Custom Cabriolet A with roadster windshield and fenders.

of the Bosch injection pump. There remained the far from inconsiderable problems of engine weight, smoother running and greater engine flexibility.

The new engine produced 45bhp at 3000rpm and was mounted on a chassis normally fitted with a 2.3-liter gasoline engine. When used in conjunction with a seven-seat limousine body, a maximum speed of 60mph was reached, the average Diesel oil consumption being 9.5 liters for 100km.

The first mass produced 260D Diesel cars were comparatively heavy since they represented a transition from the light commercial vehicle to the light passenger car. They were originally intended to be used as taxi cabs, hire cars and light delivery vans but, in practice, it turned out that this particular model was very popular in the private car class. The additional cost of more powerful selfstarters and larger capacity batteries was more than offset by the fuel economy achieved.

They were also cars built to last. A vehicle owned by a transport company in Wurttemberg was in service for thirteen years during which time it covered 808,000 miles, at one time being used to tow a cattle trailer. The engine was regularly replaced after each 155,000 miles and the rear axle after about 373,000 miles.

Quite a number of these 260D Diesel models are still in use today.

Above: This striking 1939 230S Roadster was originally owned by the Postmaster of Berlin who apparently thought so highly of it that he arranged for it to appear on a postage stamp. Now owned by Mr. Mel Melton.

Postwar recovery

Top: The rather ordinary lines of the 1952 Cabriolet 300S (109mph, 176km/h) gave little hint of the postwar classic to come. Above: The 1955 300SL with its gullwing doors was to achieve great racing success. This one is appropriately owned by former World Champion John Surtees.

TGH 25

'Daimler-Benz ceased to exist in 1945 . . . destruction to the Unterturkheim works was 70 percent, to Sindelfingen 85 percent, Mannheim 20 percent and Gaggenau 80 percent while what remained of the plant at Marienfelde was pulled down.' Such was the report of the Daimler board at the cessation of the war in Europe.

The company had to start all over again; a colossal task slightly eased by the fact that the plants at Unterturkheim, Sindelfingen and Mannheim were all in the American zone of occupation.

Staff were engaged, the debris was cleared and work was commenced. Repair, maintenance and general service work took pride of place, together with the production of commercial vehicles. But the currency reform of 1948 paved the way for a resumption of private car manufacture and the introduction of new models. Not surprisingly, production was at first confined to prewar models, notably the highly successful 170V. With business improving a development of the 170V, the 170S, was introduced and also a 1.7-liter Diesel-engined passenger car, the 170D.

Great progress was made in driving qualities, largely by a favorable distribution of weight plus suitable track dimensions. Independent suspension on a rigid frame was featured and the car's outstanding holding qualities and braking efficiency made it much in demand for police work and other specialized requirements.

Daimler-Benz had always been to the forefront in experimenting with Diesel engines and now the experience they had gained from their Diesel passenger car of 1936 was turned to good effect in order to produce a small Diesel engine which had the liveliness and the advantages of a gasoline engine. The Diesel-engined car became even more popular when it was fitted with the 170S body and rechristened the 170DS towards the end of 1952. At the same time, all the cars in the 170 range were provided with a hypoid rear axle and a wider track, thus reducing running noise and improving roadholding still further. In the case of the 170S, a new bulk synchromesh gearbox was introduced with a steering column gearshift.

Meanwhile, in 1951, the 220 was introduced. Even more than the 170S, this car combined good roadholding, soft suspensions, road safety and the speed of a large car with the economy of a middle sized one. The chassis was a strengthened and refined version of the 170S and the car was powered by a 2.2-liter engine of six cylinders, noted for its quiet running. A fully synchronized four-speed transmission was provided with a gearshift on the steering column.

The power to weight ratio of the car was a considerable improvement on the 170S and the 220 combined the qualities of a fast sportscar with those of a comfortable family car, as can be seen from the elegant lines and interior appointment of the two-seat convertible and coupé models.

The 300 model was first shown at the Frankfurt Motor Show in the spring of 1951, together with the 220, signifying a return of the tradition of rounding off the production program with a touring car of outstandingly high quality. The 300 was an elegant six-seat touring car with a six-cylinder engine capable of 100mph. Among the refinements on this car was an auxiliary rear suspension, electrically controlled, which could be operated from the driving seat and adjusted to suit the weight being carried. From 1955, the 300 was supplied with a newly developed single joint swing axle which further improved driving comfort.

During 1952 the 300 was supplemented by the two-seat 300S for those owners seeking higher performance. The 150hp engine had a higher compression ratio than in the

Below: The distinctive Mercedes personality had yet to emerge on the 1952 170 Saloon although the model sold well.
Above: The engine and (right) rear view.

300 and was equipped with three down draught carburetors. Maximum speed was said to be 110mph. Three years later this car was superseded by the 300SC, fitted with a direct gasoline injection engine and capable of 112mph. Both models were available as a convertible, coupé or roadster.

In 1953 an entirely new type of chassis was introduced. The 170V and S, 220 and 300 had X-shaped, oval tube frames. The basis of the new design was high sectional steel tubes united with the floor of the body to form a platform resistant to distortion. This method doubled rigidity besides considerably reducing noise. The subframe, which carried the complete power unit and transmission, as well as the steering and front wheel assembly, was anchored to the front part of the chassis on rubber blocks in accord with the three point suspension system. There were considerable advantages both in manufacture and in ease of maintenance and this was thought to be the first example of a design where heavy components were easily detachable.

Thus was born the 180, roomy, comfortable, economical to run and with a clear view of the road from the driver's seat, the window area being 40 percent more than in the 170S. The external lines conformed with the new pontoon design which had been adopted but the traditional Mercedes radiator

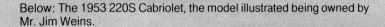

was retained. The car had a four-cylinder engine and maximum speed was 78mph.

The efficiency of the 180 range and the new chassis design was directly responsible for the introduction in 1954 of another new model, 220a, which had the same kind of chassis but an enlarged interior and increased window space. Like the earlier 220, the car had a six-cylinder engine but it was much more flexible. A different type of rear axle improved cornering, general refinement and safety and the following year this type of axle was also fitted to the 180. During the winter of 1953–4, Diesel-engined versions of both the 180 and the 220a were introduced.

Side by side with private car production, the Daimler-Benz factories produced a wide range of vans and trucks together with a complete range of municipal transport: fire engines, ambulances, road sweepers and sprinklers, refuse collectors and sewage disposal trucks.

Almost every manufacturer at one time or another has

Below: The 1953 220S Cabriolet, the model illustrated being owned by Mr. Jim Weins.

Right: Detail of the 1953 Mercedes-Benz 220 Sedan showing the somewhat conventional bodywork. Left: The more detailed steering-wheel and instrument dashboard facia.

produced some sort of novelty vehicle and sometimes these, as in the case of the British Land Rover, have turned out to be a great success. The Daimler contribution to this varied collection was the UNIMOG, a combined tractor, working machine and transporter, which from its introduction in 1948 did rather well.

Together with sports and racing car development, it added up to a very busy first postwar decade, one which no one would have thought possible as they gazed at the wreckage of the original Daimler-Benz plants.

The following decades were to be just as exciting and just as productive. One thing however would remain constant. The UNIMOG would go on and on just like the Land Rover and although various improvements were made and variations introduced this versatile vehicle would remain in demand both for military and civilian use, the high spot of its career being the first west to east crossing of the Sahara Desert in 1965.

At the 1959 Frankfurt International Automobile Exhibition a number of new Mercedes models in the 2.2-liter series were introduced. Engine design and transmission remained unchanged but substantial improvements were made in wheel suspension. The backroom workers had concentrated their attention on roadholding and driving comfort and new features included a compensating spring above the differential gear of the rear axle and shock absorbers arranged in close proximity to the wheels. The styling was rather functional, and the manufacturers themselves described the body

as 'modern but unaffected by passing trends of fashion.' A more objective eye might consider the body style to be rather unattractive.

The company's Jubilee Year, 1961, was marked by the opening of the new Daimler-Benz Museum and the opening day was chosen to announce a new model, the Mercedes-Benz 220SE coupe. The synthesis of a sports car and a utility vehicle, the new model had a 120hp injection engine and front disk brakes. Other 1961 cars included the 220SE and the 300SE, the latter having the proven 160hp engine giving a top speed of 104mph. Fully automatic transmission with hydraulic clutch, air suspension with automatic level adjustment, disk brakes with all wheel servoboost and power steer-

ing, completed the picture. The 190 range had the panorama body typical of the 220s but on the 180 range the old body styling was retained in order to keep the price down.

The basic 220S was made in large numbers but the fuel injection 220SE was a relatively scarce item. Less than 4000 were delivered in two seasons, of which cabriolets and coupes made up only 1942. One of these coupes, a 1959 version, was auctioned at the British National Motor Museum at Beaulieu in 1981. It had been supplied new to an owner in Jersey and imported into England in 1961.

The sportscar tradition continued in the range. The 230SL was unveiled in 1963 as a follow on to the 190SL and 300SL and then came the 250SL (1966), the 280SL (1967) and the 250SL (1971), the latter having a new design body and V8 engine.

With passenger car production expanding steadily and the successful reign of the 220 and 300, the company decided that the time had come for a Super Mercedes There had been two such cars prior to World War 2, the 7.7-liter eight-cylinder model and another, on similar lines, in 1938. One of the original Supers came on the market in 1962 when the famous Sword Collection in Scotland was broken up and part of it auctioned. A limousine finished in wine and black with wine upholstery and the original Daimler-Benz bodywork, it went for the bargain price of £250 (US $600).

The new Super emerged as a 6.3-liter car with eight-cylinder V engine, gasoline injection, dual circuit power braking system, disk brakes, automatic transmission, power steering, locking differential, air suspension, shock absorbers which could be adjusted while driving, hydraulic systems, electronically controlled heating, a controlled ventilation system and

Below: A 1955 300SL gullwing pictured at an auction in Auburn, Indiana. Left and below left: Rear and side views of the 300SL roadster which give an excellent picture of the beautiful streamlining which distinguished this vehicle and made it the classic Mercedes of post-war just as the SSK was between the wars.

Below: 1960 Mercedes-Benz 300 Cabriolet D with automatic transmission and power-steering. The car illustrated, one of the last 16 made, is now owned by Mr. Ralph Pennoyer.

Above: A sunroof version of the 1957 300SC Coupe with fuel injection. Below: A 1964 230 SL. Right: A 1960 300SL Roadster. The 300SL had 15,000 miles on the clock at the time of going to Press and even the tires were the original Continental racing whitewalls.

a master locking system. It was available as a six-seat limousine or in a Pullman version with three rows of seats.

The catalog described it as: 'a combination of distinction and prestige with a technical appointment which seeks its equal as regards completeness, maturity and progressiveness. As far as the design of the body is concerned, preference was given to elegance rather than fashion, an elegance the sovereign calm of which is timeless.'

The eloquence would not have won any awards from William Shakespeare, Dorothy Parker or even Damon Runyon — something was lost perhaps in translation from the original German ? — but once again we have the constant Mercedes theme of timeless and non-dating appearance and a refusal to change body styling to meet the whims of fashion.

The Model 600, as it was labelled, was certainly impressive and the Pullman version, with a dry weight of 5865lbs, was said to be the heaviest private car in production. Certainly those who drove it, presumably chauffeurs in the main, must have been glad of the power steering.

In 1963 Mercedes-Benz also took stock of themselves and their products and decided that the time had come to launch a completely new program. This was initiated the same year and brought to fruition in January 1968 after five years of research and development.

Not surprisingly there were no startling new models produced during this gestation period and most Mercedes cars between 1963 and 1968 were existing models with some improvements and refinements. This was, however, a period during which some features made astonishing progress. Notable among these was the Daimler-Benz automatic transmission, introduced in 1962, and developed especially for the firm's own passenger car production. Functioning as a hydraulic/automatic four-speed transmission it is well suited to the specific output of Mercedes-Benz engines. The hydraulic clutch, based on the Fottinger principle, transfers engine power to the selfshifting planetary gearbox without wear and with only about two percent slip, virtually nil. The gearbox has two planetary gear sets, three multiple disk clutches and three band brakes. The individual gears are controlled by a shift valve in the control unit via the pressure in the suction pipe, dependent on the engine torque, and via the pressure sensor, dependent on the driving speed.

In view of the fact that two planetary gear sets are used in the automatic transmission, it is interesting to note that Karl Benz also used two planetary gear trains in a transmission he patented in 1897 and these became a characteristic feature of a belt type planetary gearbox for three forward speeds and one reverse, offering the advantage of what was for those days exceptionally smooth gearshifting. Benz's patent refers to an epicyclic transmission for steep gradients and single lever operation for four functions – clutch operation, gearshifting, changing speed and braking. In other words, even in that pioneer period he was trying to relieve the driver of as many tasks as possible.

In the heavy traffic of today, fender to fender driving can impose exceptionally heavy wear on the conventional friction clutch but not on the automatic transmission with hydraulic clutch.

The automatic can be overridden by the sporty driver if he so wishes but the dramatic growth in the number of automatics is certainly evidence that most drivers are quite happy to accept automatic transmission and take their driving more easily. During 1962 only five out of every 100 gearboxes installed in Mercedes were automatics. By 1966 this figure had risen to 23 in 100 and five years further on, to 34.5 per 100, fulfilment of Benz's aim.

Meanwhile, as automatic transmission gained in popularity, work was nearing completion on the new range of automobiles. This was truly to be a 'New Generation' of cars.

Below: The Mercedes-Benz 450SEL. This car is the version intended for the United States market.
Right: The engine compartment of the United States version of the 280SE 4.5.

The new generation

What was termed 'The New Generation' was presented to the public in January 1968, and covered no less than fifteen models.

The innovations were many and were summarized by the manufacturers thus:

'The engines, partly further developments, partly new models, are not primarily designed to attain maximum top speeds but to produce a higher torque to help keep traffic moving and to provide quiet running and flexibility as a means of relieving the driver (of stress and fatigue).

'The interior is designed to yield on impact and to absorb shock. Even when wearing a safety belt, the foot operated parking brake which is released by a hand knob, is easy to operate and it has even been possible to attain a further improvement in the already cultivated roadholding of Mercedes-Benz passenger cars. Track and camber changes during spring travel have no adverse effects on the newly developed rear diagonal swing axle.

'As far as exterior design is concerned, the bodywork of The New Generation resembles that of the Mercedes 250S/SE of 1966, a car characterized by a long, low silhouette, low lying waistline and a very wide, low radiator grille of the traditional type . . . creating a body which will retain the fascination of elegant yet functional styling for a long time to come.'

The high performance vehicle in the new range was represented by the convertible and coupe versions of the Mercedes-Benz 280SE. In the case of this car, the company was not

Above: A detail showing the interior of the 280SE. Right: The still-improving elegance of the front end of a 1979 450SLC. Below: The very familiar shape of a 1968 280SE Saloon which, the Roadster apart, is very much the type of automobile with which the public associates Mercedes-Benz.

only concerned with providing a fast and exclusive car but also with meeting all the safety demands resulting from a higher speed range. Here too, therefore, the engineers adhered to the proven design principle of a running gear adapted to suit the full engine power. An efficient braking system was also essential for drivers who wanted to maintain high average speeds, a car being only as fast as its brakes. Twin circuit disk brakes were installed on the 280SE and thanks to vacuum control these required the minimum of effort on the part of the driver. A brake pressure control, of which more later, prevented the brakes from locking.

A newly developed 3.5-liter V8 engine was available for both the convertible and the coupé and three years later was also made available for the 280SE and SEL limousines and as an alternative to the 6.3-liter V engine for the 300SEL. With a bore of 92mm and a stroke of 65.8mm, the engine was of the short stroke type but had an exceptionally high engine speed thanks to the provision of one overhead camshaft per row of cylinders.

The engine developed 6500rpm and so was ideal for sporty driving. Fuel was fed to the cylinders via an electronically controlled injection unit similar to that of the 250CE coupé. This unit was installed between the cylinder heads in order to save space, thus helping to make the engine low. The transistorized ignition system represented another step forward. Apart from improved ignition efficiency, the main advantage was that the contact breaker points were only subjected to stress from the low control current of the transistor unit, thus avoiding contact burn off and a change in the ignition timing.

Of course, the company had no intention of resting on its 'New Generation' laurels. The guide lines had been laid down and within that framework more innovations came along.

Major changes were made to the saloon and estate cars in 1976 with the W123 compact bodied saloons ranging from 200 to 280E. The 200 had a four-cylinder 2-liter gasoline engine of 94hp; there was also a four-cylinder 2-liter Diesel engined version, the 200D, and the 240D, which had a 2.4-liter Diesel engine. The others in this range were the 230 (four-cylinder 2.3-liter, gasoline, 109hp); 300D (five-cylinder 3-liter, Diesel, 80hp); 250 (six-cylinder 2.15-liter, gasoline,

Above, below and right: The Mercedes-Benz 450SLC from all angles. Some 54,000 SLCs were built during the period 1972 to 1980 and the car illustrated is a 1979 version. The distinctive three-pointed star can be guaranteed to attract attention!

129hp); and 280E (six-cylinder 2.8-liter, gasoline, 185hp).

Three years later came estate car versions of some of these models, two Diesel powered and two running on gasoline: 240TD, 300TD, 250T and 280TE.

A New S-class of saloon cars was introduced to the left-hand drive market and later to the UK market, where they made their debut at the first International Motor Show to be held at Britain's Birmingham exhibition complex in 1980. All three models had gasoline engines, the 280SE having a six-cylinder power unit of 185hp while the 380SE and the 500SE both had V8 engines, one of 218hp and the other of 240hp.

Changes took place too in the sportscar and coupes. 1977 brought the 230C coupe (four-cylinder 2.3-liter, gasoline, 109hp) and the 280CE coupe (six-cylinder 2.8-liter, gasoline, 185hp). In 1980 came the 380SL two-seat (V8 3.8-liter, gasoline, 118hp); 380SLC (a coupé version of the same car with fixed head); and the 500SL two-seat (V8 5-liter, 240hp).

Other significant improvements were made to existing models in 1980 which included new and more powerful four-cylinder engines for the 200 (109hp) and 230 (136hp). The 230 now had a designation of 230E meaning that fuel injection was employed and the same engine was fitted in the 230CE coupé and the 230TE estate car. The 200T estate car became available with an uprated 2-liter engine.

It should be noted that in the United States different speci-

Above: United States' version of the 280SE 4.5. Top right: Detail of the 280 SE's driving compartment. Top left: The more sporty lines of a 1969 Mercedes 250SL, seen parked in the street at Fort Wayne, Indiana.

fications apply but that due to the straightforward coding system employed by Mercedes it is easy to work out exactly what the models are: for instance, 300CD is a coupe, Diesel-powered, and 300SD is an S-class saloon with turbo Diesel.

Successive models have continued to improve in the sphere of quiet running, a smooth ride and lack of engine vibration. Comfort is also a feature of the sporty Mercedes roadsters which to traditionalists, may seem a contradiction in terms. One of the few cars in the world today to offer the pleasures of 'open top' motoring, the roadster is available with a completely disappearing soft top or a removable steel hard top. These roadsters were the first cars in the world to be offered with their doors 'plumbed in' to the heating system so that warm air can be circulated around the occupants, an important point in an open car.

The four/five-seat sports coupe has fixed head and is some 14 inches longer in order to accommodate the extra row of seats. Even here, a typical refinement is introduced with a special lock which fixes the backs of the front seats in place when the doors are closed and the engine is running. And, although the marque is not so active in competition work as in earlier times, the four/five-seat has a good record in long distance international rallies. Mercedes sportscars are very popular in the United States which is the premier export market for them with Great Britain second and Japan a very bad third.

In recent years, the company has also marketed the 'T series' of estate cars, built at the Bremen works and available in a variety of engine sizes: 2, 2.3 and 2.8-liter gasoline engines and 2.4 and 3-liter Diesel. The hallmark of the manufacturer is also on these vehicles with power assisted steering

Above and right: The Mercedes-Benz 450SEL, US version: three shots of this car showing the entire vehicle, detail of the steering wheel, seats and driving compartment, and under the hood.

and central locking for all five doors as standard. The tailgate opens and closes easily with the help of a concealed gasfilled strut support. The rear window is equipped with washer and wiper. Other features include a self levelling device in the rear axle to ensure a level ride whatever the load; a rolling blind and parcels net installed behind the rear seats; and twin chromium rails on the roof. A divided rear bench seat and extra foldaway childrens' seats in the rear compartment are optional.

Another proven series is the 'G' four-wheel drive crosscountry vehicles which come in short and long wheelbase versions with either six-cylinder gasoline injection engines (280GE) or five-cylinder Diesel units. Unlike many light crosscountry vehicles, automatic transmission is available. The big technical development in this series is the provision of 100 percent differential locks on both axles. These can be engaged or disengaged while on the move and impart an extraordinary degree of crosscountry ability to the vehicle. For normal roadgoing purposes, only two-wheel drive is required but the addition of a differential lock means that quite difficult terrain can be tackled without resorting to four-wheel drive. When the going gets really tough, however, a crosscountry ratio of 2.74:1, combined with differential locks on both axles, means that forward progress can be maintained as long as one wheel remains in contact with firm ground. As with the differential locks, the crosscountry ratio can be engaged while on the move.

Above: The latest in Mercedes energy – engine of the 1983 500SEC.
Top: Sturdy construction for safety is epitomised by Diesel-powered 1935
260D limousine.

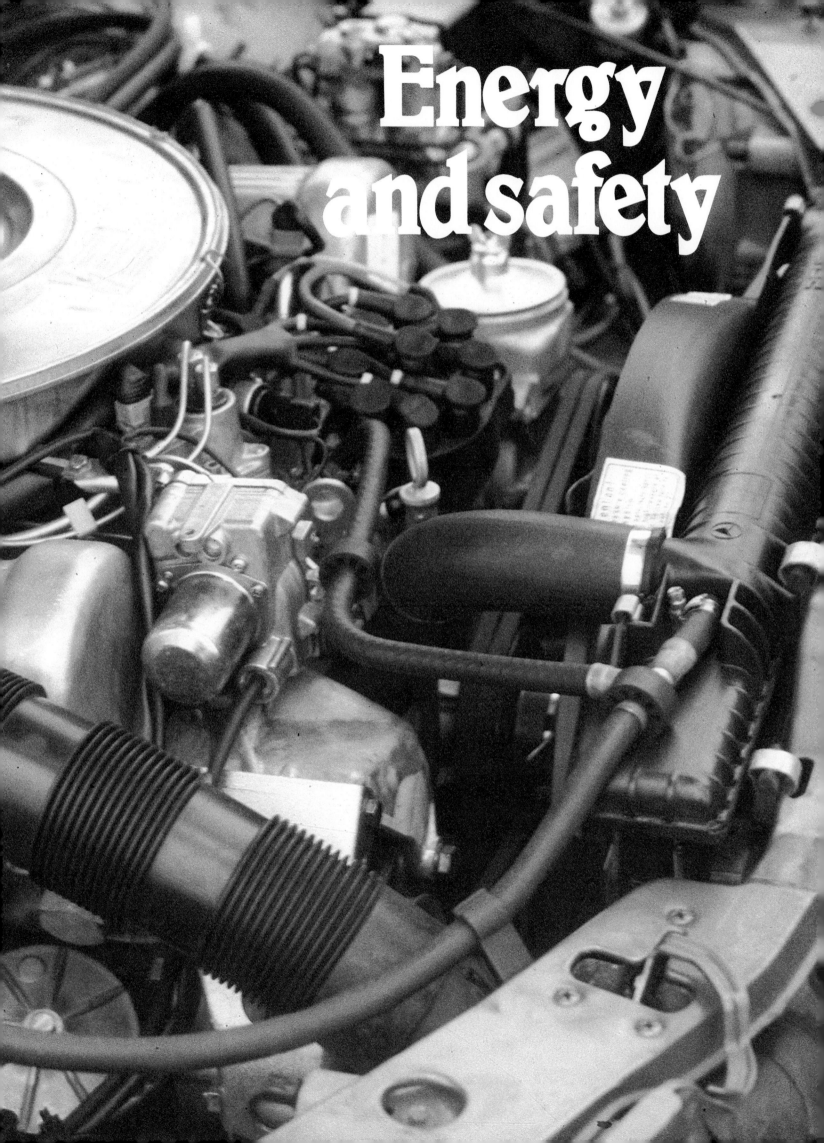

Energy and safety

From the introduction of what was claimed to be the first Diesel engined private car to be marketed, the 260D in 1936, Daimler-Benz have paid more attention to fuel economy than their general public image as makers of large, fast and fairly expensive automobiles would indicate. Perhaps the most significant step was the development of the commercial Diesel engine to the point where it became, with a steady increase in speed and a reduction of running noise, a feasible project for the family car and highly desirable for the taxi. The already basic economy was then further improved by means of direct injection, long before direct injection was featured in high performance gasoline engined cars.

Then, in the fifties, in collaboration with the Robert Bosch company, Mercedes developed a fuel injection system for gasoline driven cars which managed to combine improved performance with what the manufacturers described as 'extremely economical' fuel consumption.

Thus, when the energy crisis hit the world, Mercedes engineers had been working on the problem for years and in 1981 the company proudly introduced Energy Concept.

Energy Concept was the reply of one manufacturer to outside pressure to make cars less demanding of the world's dwindling fuel supplies, and it introduced a number of modifications designed to reduce fuel consumption. The cars involved had 'EC' added to the model code, for example, 380SEC and 500SEC.

In striving for economy, the company brought in new 'high technology' light alloy engines and also paid a great deal of attention to body weight. Streamlining was also very much in the picture and the 'EC' cars unveiled at the Frankfurt Motor Show in 1981 showed unmistakable signs of extensive research in the wind tunnels.

The most evident change concerned the radiator aperture and grille which sloped upward and to the rear, presenting a smoother shape to the air flow over the body than the former downward sloping design. Chief Stylist Bruno Sacco commented briefly: 'The shark's mouth has given way to the laid back look in the cause of better aerodynamics.'

Weight had been reduced by using light alloy for the trunk lid, hood and rear bulkhead. The four-speed torque converter automatic transmission improved economy by offering an optimum spread of ratios and, said Mercedes, 'by listening to the driver's foot.' A manual five-speed transmission followed, the top gear of which was a high or economy ratio.

Other measures taken included reducing idle speeds, introducing fuel cut off on the overrun, raising of compression to improve combustion and faster warm up from cold. In the case of the 3.8-liter V8 engine, the bore and stroke were altered.

All sorts of other avenues were explored including power losses caused by secondary units. The successful results were applied across the range and not only to the 'EC' models although, of course, the amount of improvement varied from model to model and depended upon the extent to which indi-

Above: A car nearing perfection: the 1982/3 500SEC Coupe. 'EC' stands for Energy Concept 'to make cars less demanding of the world's dwindling fuel supplies'.

vidual designs could be modified. The lowest improvement claimed in fuel consumption was 3 percent, the highest 23 percent.

In terms of figures, the steps taken with aerodynamics coupled with the extensive use of light alloys and high tensile sheet steel, apart from making the cars lighter, reduced the drag coefficient by 14 percent. Yet door and seat heights, interior width and the visibility of all four corners of the car were maintained or improved. Commented Friedrich van Winsen, head of car development: 'Mere downsizing as it is done everywhere else was out of the question for Mercedes. For us, reduction in fuel consumption could only be achieved by technically more sophisticated measures.'

These measures led to dramatic weight saving in the cases of the big 3.8-liter and 5-liter V8 engines, something of the order of up to 280 kilograms. The new V8s also featured improved thermodynamic and mechanical efficiency, all contributing to greater economy. The torque converter four-speed automatic transmission performed automatically all those functions which in a five-speed manual transmission require the driver's special attention and 'feel' if he is to select the highest and therefore most economical gear possible.

The average reduction in fuel consumption was more than 10 percent, a considerable achievement since it was claimed that the 2.8-liter car now performed like the former 3.5 and the 3.8-liter light alloy V8 had an equivalent performance to the former 4.5 cast iron 450SE. The performance of the previous top model in the range, the 450SEL 6.9-liter, had been matched with a smaller and much lighter 5-liter engine.

The fuel consumption figures according to the EEC norm show that these generously proportioned long distance touring cars could cover the ground fairly economically as well as comfortably.

	Town	56mph	75mph
280SE	16.7	30.0	24.1
380SEL	15.0	25.4	21.2
500SEL	12.9	24.9	20.8

Apart from economy, automobile manufacturers in recent years have been under great pressure to make cars safer. Campaigners such as Ralph Nader have directed the spotlight of publicity on the matter and the outcome has been much stricter measures concerning safety, notably in the United States but also in the European Community and in other countries.

So, side by side with their research into fuel economy, or perhaps fuel efficiency would be a better description, Mercedes scientists, engineers, draughtsmen and stylists have been hunting to find ways of building safer cars and equipping them with additional safety devices.

There are obvious limits to the developments in the field of fuel economy or efficiency, limits beyond which it is impossible to go without seriously damaging performance. Other than cost, there are no such limits in the field of safety and Mercedes can claim with some justification to be among

Below and left: Pride of the marque: Mercedes-Benz 500SEC of 1983 in all its aspects including details of the seating and interior. The photograph near right shows the seatbelt fitment which 'offers' the belt to the driver and front seat passenger when the ignition is turned on.

the foremost manufacturers in introducing safety features on their vehicles. Safety is a design principle as far as they are concerned, a principle which demands not only scientific investigation but investigation of all component parts.

They put safety under two headings, *Active* and *Passive*. Active safety comprises those measures which serve to *prevent* accidents and thus promote driving safety. These measures include individual wheel suspension at both the front and rear; a wide track; low lying center of gravity; light recirculating ball steering; steering dampers; effective dual circuit braking system with power boost; and disk brakes which can be subjected to high thermal stress. The driver's wellbeing is very much a part of active safety so this means comfortable springing, coupled with excellent roadholding, effective damping of vibration and all kinds of road and other noises, seat springing, a good allround view and windshield wipers which cover a large area. It is also essential to arrange switches and knobs so that they are readily accessible to the driver but not to anyone else, for example, small children. They must also be so designed, marked and positioned that they cannot be confused one with another.

Before delving deeper into active safety let us be clear on what is meant by passive safety.

This encompasses those measures which mitigate or even eliminate the effects of an accident. Interior and exterior design are both important in this context. The body should be impact reducing with effective bumpers, rounded door handles, smooth wheel hub caps and no sharp projections such as radiator mascots. Front and rear sections should be capable of absorbing considerable impact. The passenger compartment should be rigid but the steering wheel should have a yielding impact absorber under a padded boss and a telescopically collapsing steering column. There should be safety locks on all doors, especially cars in which children travel, windows of laminated glass, a yielding instrument panel, padded door pillars and arm rests, flush fitted door handles, flexible grab handles, padded and adjustable sun vizors and a protected fuel tank.

Mercedes claim an outstanding 'first' under this heading as the first company to introduce progressive crumpling safety cell bodywork, the theory of which is that in a collision the bodywork crumples around the driver and passengers who remain protected in the toughest compartment of the vehicle. Many a person has been killed in an auto accident because part of the bodywork did not crumple and so either crushed or pierced their bodies or trapped them in the wreckage.

Prevention being better than cure, Mercedes also claim a 'first' in the field of active safety as the first company to have introduced antilock braking into series production. Many manufacturers might offer such a system on the top end of their range, Mercedes offer it across the entire range. Engineers at Stuttgart began work on such a system more than twenty years ago and have since worked with Bosch on developing it. The system was first demonstrated publicly in 1969 but was not released for production until ten years later, evidence of the painstaking care which goes into such innovations. The ABS antilock braking system, as it is known, developed jointly by Bosch and Daimler-Benz AG, made its debut on the 500SE and SEL models and was available as an optional extra on the 280SE, 380SE and SEL. It is now available on each new car to be introduced.

Few drivers can have avoided the terrifying experience of being forced to brake on a wet or icy road, perhaps by a sudden or unexpected obstruction or a pedestrian darting across the road, and then finding themselves in a dangerous skid. The lucky majority live to tell the tale but an unfortunate minority are wiped out by a truck or some other vehicle or by collision with what planners call 'street furniture.'

When the brakes are slammed on and the driver attempts to change direction, the road wheels tend to lock: and a locked road wheel cannot change direction. So the car slides on out of control. *But* the road wheel that is still rotating can be steered. That is what the antilock system is all about. With such a system fitted, the driver can brake hard, take evasive action and still be in control of the vehicle in any road conditions, at any speed and under any load.

As well as reducing stopping distances on wet or icy roads by as much as 40 percent, the system enables the driver to retain full steering control even during 'panic braking.' On even a novice driver it confers automatically the rally driver's skill in 'cadence braking,' the technique used by experts to retain steering control during heavy braking. The expert rally driver brakes in a series of hard dabs on the brake pedal until the wheels *almost* reach locking point. In between each 'dab' he releases the brake pedal so that the wheels begin to revolve again before he reapplies the brakes. Even this, done properly (and few can do it) cannot measure up to the Mercedes ABS system which does the same thing, only electronically and faster. Also, with 'cadence braking' the deceleration on all four wheels is equal whereas the ABS system can deal with one recalcitrant wheel.

Three speed sensors, one on each front wheel and the third for both rear wheels, tell the central control unit when the wheel is about to lock. Instructions are given by the control unit to the hydraulic brake unit and carried out by three highly responsive magnetic valves. Pressure in the hydraulic lines is then reduced so that the wheel begins to turn again. As soon as it reaches a predetermined rate, brake pressure is reapplied. The timing is controlled by a quartz crystal. The result is that the wheels keep turning rather than locking and the car remains fully steerable throughout.

Since the sensors are measuring with great accuracy whether or not all the wheels are rotating at the correct speed at every moment during deceleration, if the speed of only one wheel becomes too low, the brake pressure is momentarily relaxed on that wheel and on that wheel only. The wheel then speeds up. When it starts to rotate too quickly then brake pressure is applied on it again. This all happens very quickly, between four and ten times a second.

The device represents probably the most significant advance in braking technology since the advent of the four-wheel hydraulically operated brake system in the 1930s and since the availability of race tested disk brakes of the 1950s.

What the ABS system *cannot* do, of course, is to defy the laws of physics and the braking distance on a wet road will always be longer than on a dry one.

Mercedes themselves reinforce the warning; 'The antilock braking system cannot help a driver *who has already exceeded the maximum speed of a corner*. Nor can it melt ice.'

The company sees the system as another form of insurance. You may never need it but it will be well worth its cost if you do. In the heavy traffic congestion of today, even expert drivers can expect sooner or later to be confronted with an emergency. A spin off is that by eliminating skidding, flat spots on tires are avoided and tire wear considerably reduced. And, of course, an accident avoided means a saving in garage bills and the maintenance of insurance premiums at a reasonable level.

The benefits therefore would seem to far outweigh the cost (at the time of writing) of approximately US $1500 (£830 sterling).

In the field of passive safety there is, of course, controversy worldwide on the subject of driver and passenger restraints. Mercedes, as might be expected, have done considerable research on the subject and have come up with some ingenious ideas although safety experts differ on the efficacy of some of them.

In 1981 the company introduced a new type of seat belt fitment. As soon as the driver and frontseat passenger are seated, the doors closed and the ignition switched on, an extending arm proffers seatbelts to them at shoulder height. The arm 'waits' for thirty seconds before gliding discreetly away. If the belt is not fitted within that thirty seconds, perhaps because the occupants are looking at a map or something of that nature – the arm will represent the belt again on the ignition being switched off momentarily. This device is available on the 380SEC and 500SEC coupes, which have no central pillar.

These pillarless coupes also present other safety problems, especially in the roof support area. High strength tube is welded into the front windshield pillars and the roof frame structure is strengthened by the addition of a gusset plate on the front corners. These measures have secured a 15 percent improvement in tests when cars have been dropped on their roofs.

Perhaps the most controversial safety measure in the world of automobiles today is the airbag, a type of which is available on Mercedes Class S Saloons as an optional extra. The airbag is mounted in the hub of the steering wheel and offers additional protection to the driver in the event of a crash. Should there be a collision an electronic device triggers off a gas propellant which inflates the bag within split seconds and cushions the head and shoulders of the driver from impact against the steering wheel and/or the windshield.

Much research has been carried out on the subject in the United States and Japan but in general the American experiments have not produced solid evidence in favor of the idea. Baboons used in experiments instead of humans have been killed and injured and in some cases the bags have failed to activate. Nor are the bags much use in side or rear collisions or when a secondary impact takes place. There is also the frightening possibility of the bag inflating accidentally while the car is traveling at speed. Some systems are said to be harmful to the hearing.

However, Mercedes themselves have carried out 2000 tests over a period of ten years and say that random firings of the devices on volunteers have shown no 'serious' adverse effects, 'serious' being their word. The company has, of course, considered all the pro's and cons and their system incorporates a monitoring circuit which constantly checks.

A warning light informs the driver if the system is functioning or not.

Since the airbag, as mentioned earlier, is an optional extra, no one has to have one if they don't want one, unlike the seatbelt which is becoming compulsory in more and more countries.

The Mercedes 'safety package' incorporates a seatbelt tensioning device, intended to ensure that the front seat passenger is correctly held by his belt. Another feature which must help to promote readier acceptance of seatbelts is that on some models the belts for the front seat occupants are adjustable for height via a three position control on the central pillar. This is a device which all manufacturers would do well to adopt since so often people are seen with belts fitted at the wrong height for them and thus so positioned that they are likely to break the unfortunate person's neck should there be a collision.

Certainly, there is enough in the Mercedes 'safety package' to indicate that the company is the leader in this field, or nearly so, and this strong emphasis on safety, both active and passive, is one of the major attractions of the marque.

Right: Inside the engine compartment of a Mercedes-Benz 280SE. This again is a version designed for the US market.

Above: Racing has always been used to 'improve the breeds'. Famed American driver, Barney Oldfield, driving the 'Lightning Benz' at Daytona Beach in 1910. Top: Luigi Fagioli (Mercedes-Benz) leads Soffietti (Maserati) in the 1935 Monaco Grand Prix.

Improving the breed

It has often been said that motor racing and rallying have 'improved the breed'; that through lessons learned on the race circuits and rally stages, manufacturers of ordinary automobiles have been able to improve the product. Although this theory is sometimes challenged in modern times there is no doubt that quite a lot of features were developed through motor sport – even the rearview mirror was first used, as far as is known, on Ray Harroun's winning Marmon in the Indianapolis 500 Mile Race of 1911. Certainly, Daimler and Benz and Mercedes introduced many innovations by way of the race tracks of the world.

Daimler's early engines were tested and proved in competition. The world's first race, or so some claim, from Paris to Rouen in 1894, was won by a cluster of Peugeots and Panhards powered with Daimler three and four horsepower engines The master himself was there and was delighted. The following year in the race from Paris to Bordeaux and back, a distance of 740 miles, cars fitted with Daimler engines filled all the leading places save fifth, a position occupied by Emile Roger, in a Benz.

That year the term 'automobile' was first used and the first Italian motor sport event held. It was won by Daimler. In Great Britain in 1900, the great Thousand Miles Trial was held and Benz and Daimler both won Manufacturers Awards, the only woman driver, Mrs Bazalgette, winning a Silver Medal in a Benz Ideal.

The advent of the Mercedes 35 demonstrated how improved gearshifting could make driving easier and performance better. Wilhelm Werner drove a 35 to victory in the 1901 Nice-Salon-Nice race and it was generally agreed that the car's positive gearshift made the work of a racing driver much easier.

Then the 1903 Gordon Bennett race, held in Ireland, saw the birth, almost by accident, of the competition sportscar. Mercedes prepared a team of pure racing cars for this prestigious event but they were destroyed in a fire at the factory

and there was no time to build replacements. The only solution was to 'race tune' some standard 60hp tourers and this was done. The Belgian driver, Camille 'The Red Devil' Jenatzy, drove one of these stripped down touring cars to racing victory and so was born the first competition sportscar.

The advent of the French Grand Prix, followed in due time by Grand Prix races in other countries, exercised the ingenuity of motoring engineers and at this time many of the steps they took to improve the performance of racing cars ultimately benefited the private car.

In 1908 a special Mercedes racing car was designed for the Grand Prix. In accordance with the formula governing the race, cylinder bore was limited to 155mm but cubic capacity was unlimited. The resulting Mercedes engine produced 135bhp at 1400rpm. An unusual feature of the car was that the equal size front and rear wooden wheels were fitted with Michelin detachable rims.

Below: Probably the most famous racing car of the early days, the 'Blitzen Benz' as it was streamlined in 1911. Above: Benz ready to race at Savannah in 1910. Savannah was an early home of the US Grand Prix.

Christian Lautenschlager drove one of these cars to win at a speed of 68.9mph, the only man in motor racing history to drive his first race in the premier event of the year and win it. Previously he had been a riding mechanic in the works team. Mercedes had a good day as their No 1 driver, Salzer, set a lap record of 78.6mph.

The race had, however, a more important lesson for all manufacturers. Cars were not allowed to practise beforehand for fear of damaging the road surfaces. No one sought to protect the cars from the roads. In the event, the race proved to be a veritable massacre of tires, the winner having used his last available spare when he crossed the line. It led to special research on racing tires, research which was to prove of benefit in leading to better quality and better designed tires for ordinary use.

The GP races before World War 1 also sounded the death knell for chain drive although a few manufacturers continued to make such cars for a long time to come. The Mercedes 'Pilettes' entered for the 1913 Grand Prix de France at Le Mans and named after the company's Belgian agent, were the last Grand Prix cars to use chain drive.

A new Mercedes GP car was designed for the 1914 French Grand Prix which was to be held at Lyons. The racing formula for that year limited the engine capacity to 4.5 liters

but using experience gained in aircraft engine production, Daimler designers and engineers built a new engine which produced 115bhp at 3200rpm. This engine speed, which could be maintained for a long time, was considered very high.

Lautenschlager won again with team mates Wagner and Salzer second and third, the first time in GP history that cars of the same marque filled the first three places.

Undoubtedly a big factor in the win was the ability to maintain a high constant speed, something which would never be overlooked in future Mercedes cars. These new engines had four cylinders, bore 93mm, stroke 165mm, and each cylinder had two overhead inlet and exhaust valves, actuated by an overhead camshaft and rocker arms. But the unique factor was that the steel cylinders had water jackets of sheet steel welded to them, a system the Daimler engineers had devised in building an aircraft engine to compete for the Kaiser's Prize. (Daimler did not win the prize – Benz did).

Mercedes also worked on good acceleration and climbing ability and just how well they accomplished this is demonstrated by their record in hill climbs. Although Wilhelm Bauer, the first ever to be killed on a hill climb, and Count Eliot Zborowski met their deaths in Mercedes, E T. Stead became the first Englishman to win a Continental hill climb

driving a Mercedes and Hermann Braun won the Austrian Semmering event four years in succession, also in a Mercedes.

At this time, Mercedes found the race track not only to be a good publicity medium, increasing the sales of their private cars, but also profitable in some cases.

In 1907, first year of racing at the new Brooklands race track in England, Mercedes ended the season as the top moneywinner with a total of about US $15,000 (£2800 sterling) which in those days represented a year's wages for more than fifty men. Napier, with £1760 and Darracq, with £1000, came next.

In the United States, despite the 1906 failure of Sartori to gain the World Land Speed Record at Daytona Beach, driving Vanderbilt's twin-engined Mercedes Special, the Italian-American Ralph de Palma was proving himself a very accomplished race driver at the wheel of a Mercedes. In 1912, he won the Vanderbilt Cup, crossing the line with one tire flat, and finished the season as American Automobile Association champion. Three years later, driving one of the Mercedes designed for the 1914 French Grand Prix, he won the classic Indianapolis 500 Mile Race at a speed of 89.84mph. De Palma's racing career was to span 27 years.

The twenties and thirties were to be great times for Merce-

Some great pioneer racers. Above far left: Wishart at the wheel of a 1912 Mercedes. Above left: The superbly-beautiful Mercedes racer of 1914, capable of 112mph (180km/h). Above: Lautenschlager, twice winner of the French GP pre-Great War, at the wheel of the 1913 7½-liter racing car. Left: Mulford at Indianapolis in 1913.

des where racing was concerned. Technically the firm made great strides but sometimes the cost, in human life, was high.

Both Daimler and Benz returned to international motor sport in 1921. A Benz sports car won the Avus race that year and the following season a 16/50 was campaigned successfully. In 1923 the Benz dropshaped racing car with a rear swing axle made its appearance and won at Monza. It proved to be the forerunner of a design which led to the floating type of axle.

In Sicily, the historic Targa Florio was soon back on the calendar and in 1921 Mercedes were given an unexpected boost when an Italian driver, Masetti, took the checkered flag in his privately entered Mercedes. It encouraged the factory to send a works team the following year but the best they could manage was sixth place, Masetti saving the day by winning for the second successive year. It was a bitter pill for the works to bow to a privateer and back in Germany the competitions department decided to give the Targa a miss for a year while they worked on a new car. Paul Daimler, Gottlieb's son, set to work to design the car and later Ferdinand Porsche added the final touches to the development of a novel supercharger installation.

Meanwhile, the Italian GP of 1923 had become the first major epreuve to be won by a supercharged car, a foretaste of things to come. The winning car was the Fiat 805. Fourth and fifth were two of the remarkable rear engined Benz Tropfenrennwagenen but despite their impressive performance it would be 1958 before Stirling Moss in a Cooper would notch up the first Grand Prix victory for a rear engine car. (The successful Auto Unions of the 1930s were mid-engined, the driver sitting in the nose.)

Above: Continuing the tradition: the stubby-tailed 1923 racer with many extraneous bits and pieces removed.
Left: The super streamlining of the Thirties – the 205mph (330km/h) of the 1937 racer.
Below: The Mercedes team lined-up before the start of the 1934 French Grand Prix. The W25s were the first race cars to carry the Mercedes-Benz name.

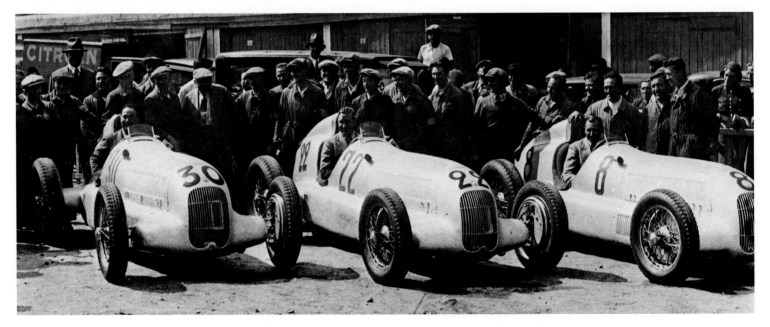

The new Mercedes soon proved its worth, Christian Werner winning the 1924 Targa at the fastest speed up to that time. But for most of the twenties and early thirties, Mercedes competition laurels were to come mainly from sports car racing and hill climbs. Grand Prix was the preserve of Bugatti, Delage and Alfa Romeo and although Mercedes did win some races labelled 'Grand Prix' they would have been more accurately termed 'Formula Libre' or, in some cases, 'Sports Car' events.

The best known Mercedes of all time, the SSK roadster with racing performance, together with its shorter wheelbase version, were the leading cars in this activity and two drivers, Rudi Caracciola and Hans Stuck, played major roles. In 1930 Stuck won the newly instituted European Mountain Championship for racing cars and Caracciola the sports car equivalent. Caracciola and Team Manager Alfred Neubauer represented almost all Daimler-Benz AG's racing commitment at this time but they were doing rather well — 180,000 marks in winnings in 1931.

In 1932 the depression caused the directors to withdraw officially from racing. Caracciola went to Alfa Romeo, only temporarily as it proved, but Neubauer contrived to enter two 'private' Mercedes in the Avus race. Although Stuck set a lap record of 125mph, it was newcomer von Brauchitsch who won. It was a significant victory in technical terms. The car was an ordinary SSKL but it had a specially designed body

which made it look like a big cigar, the first glimpse Berlin had had of 'streamline'.

It says something for Neubauer and his drivers — Caracciola, Stuck, von Brauchitsch and poor Christian Werner who died of cancer of the throat in 1932 — and even more for the redoubtable SSK that Mercedes stayed in the front rank of motor sport competition for a nine year period during which Daimler-Benz AG *did not produce a single out and out racing car.* Among their successes during that time were Caracciola's win in the 1926 German Grand Prix, a race he was to win six times; victory in the 1930 Irish Grand Prix; and again in the Mille Miglia, Caracciola being the first non-Italian to win this classic race.

In a short wheelbase SSK 38/250 supercharged 7-liter, Werner and Caracciola put up an epic struggle at Le Mans during which they broke the lap record before being forced to retire. The following year, Stoffel and Ivanowsky managed second place in a similar car.

Paul Daimler's eight-cylinder 2-liter supercharged racer was not manufactured after 1925 and it was to be 1934 before a Mercedes-Benz racing car would be unveiled. The new car was built to the 750kg formula which was to govern Grand Prix racing from 1934 to 1936 and eventually to be extended to 1937. Under this formula, the weight of the car, excluding driver, tires and fuel, could not exceed 750kg, irrespective of engine power. The W25, as it was designated, had an eight-cylinder in line engine with front mounted supercharger and two pressure carburetors. It's effectiveness can be judged by the fact that speeds of up to 185mph, depending upon the gear ratio, were reached with open cars in road races; and records of up to 280mph were set by streamlined versions of the car. Driven by von Brauchitsch, the W25 won the Eifelrennen at the Nurburgring on its first time out and thus became the first racing car fitted with independent suspension all round to win a race. The fiery Italian driver, Luigi Fagioli, had a rapport with the W25, winning the Spanish, Italian, and Pescara GPs plus the Coppa Acerbo in one season and the Monaco, German and Spanish GPs the next.

On the Avus circuit, the W25 recorded 193.85mph over a flying mile and at Gyon, near Budapest, set a number of world records during which the car attained a maximum speed of 199.36mph. It took the one mile standing start record at an average speed of 117.19mph.

An improved version of the car, the W125, was brought out for the 1937 season and was noteworthy in several respects not least in that it incorporated a feature which had first been used on private cars, a reversal of the usual process. The W125 closely resembled its predecessor but the method of controlling the thrust of the rear wheels was entirely different. The innovation ensured that the rear wheels kept their track and that the thrust and braking momentum were transmitted to the frame by means of side members. In other words, the secret was that the De Dion rear axle, *conceived in*

Above: Pre-war power at Pau in 1957.
Above right: The record-breaking W125 of 1938, capable of 270mph (433km/h).
Below: The 1954 Formula One racer, designed for 186mph (300km/h).

the nineteenth century, had at last been introduced to motor racing. During the next two decades its use would become widespread.

The W125 was the most powerful Grand Prix car ever built, its supercharged 5.66-liter straight eight engine producing over 600bhp (646bhp in bench tests). It had only one foot operated four-wheel hydraulic brake and there was no handbrake. Raced for only one season, because of the change in formula in 1938, the W125 won seven of the twelve races in which it started and was an even bigger success than the W25. Mechanic turned driver, Hermann Lang, won the fastest race of the season, on the Avus track, at a speed of 162.6mph. He had previously won the Tripoli Grand Prix.

On 28 January 1938 Caracciola, driving a twelve-cylinder 5.57-liter Mercedes racing car with streamlined body, set an international class record for the kilometer with an average speed of 268.9mph on the Frankfurt-Darmstadt autobahn. was timed in one direction at 271.5mph. The record is still unbeaten at the time of writing and remains the highest speed ever attained on a public road.

The 750kg (1655lbs) formula had been replaced by one which limited the cubic capacity of supercharged engines to 3 liters and stipulated a minimum weight limit of 850kg (1874lbs). The 3-liter Mercedes, W154, built to the formula. had a chassis very similar to the W25 and W125 but, learning from past experience, they had a much lower center of gravity to improve roadholding, something which Mercedes have since concentrated on in building passenger cars. The V12 engine had a cubic capacity of 2962 and was designed to attain 7800rpm and produce more than 480bhp. There were two parallel superchargers mounted on the front of the engine. (For 1939 a two stage supercharger was to be used).

Apart from the cars, it had become increasingly obvious through the years that Mercedes had an outstanding team manager in Neubauer who is generally credited with being the man to introduce a proper code of signals from the pits to drivers during a race, a system subsequently adopted universally and still in use today.

The drivers were great but temperamental. Von Brauchitsch looked down on Lang for his proletarian origins, Lang had to be restrained from breaking up cars by driving flat out, the Englishman Dick Seaman usually had the uneasy role of peacemaker, and the great Caracciola suffered from worms. Lang's wife was supersitious and so was Caracciola's. Seaman would never occupy Room 13 or drive a car with that number. No matter, Neubauer could handle them all.

Below: The 1952 300SL in trim for the Central and South American road races. The car could do 161mph (260km/h).

The cars were also great but temperamental. They had to have special racing oil, as tough as rubber, which stood half the night on a stove before it could be poured in. Then there were special plugs for warming up. After that the hoods were covered with blankets, like race horses, to prevent them cooling off. Finally racing plugs were put in which would function only at a certain temperature and which at low speed would become oiled up. The fuel had to be mixed according to the weather.

In 1938, Lang won in Tripoli, von Brauchitsch in France, Seaman took the German GP, Caracciola the Swiss. Caracciola won the Coppa Acerbo and Lang the Coppa Ciano. At the end of the season, Caracciola, worms and all, was European Champion for the third time (there was no World Championship at that time).

The 1939 season was to bring a true test of the design and engineering ability of Daimler-Benz AG. The Grand Prix cars were to be much the same as for 1938, apart from the supercharger modification already mentioned. Then the Italians sprung a surprise.

Smarting under the indignity of not winning a single Grand Prix during 1938 (the Italian Grand Prix had gone to the other German team, Auto Union), the Italian Sporting Commission announced that the 1939 Tripoli Race would be confined to 1.5 liter cars, a class which had always been dominated by the Italians and French.

Daimler-Benz had less than eight months in which to meet the challenge and in this time they designed, built and tested an eight-cylinder car, the W165. Then they went to North Africa and took first and second places through Lang and Caracciola. Lang went on to win the Eifelrennen, the Belgian and Swiss Grands Prix and the Grand Prix of Pau. At the end of the season he had succeeded Caracciola as European Champion and had also won the European Mountain Championship. It was another great year for Mercedes but marred by the death of Seaman in the Belgian race. In September, Neubauer, Lang and von Brauchitsch were in Belgrade for the last race of the season when the news came that German troops had invaded Poland.

In looking at Mercedes' racing achievements in the 1930s one must not be led into thinking that only one type of engine was produced to each formula. Between 1934 and 1939 it was estimated that the racing department at Stuttgart produced something like twenty different engines and major modifications, some of which were not raced and some of which were used only for record purposes. Others were put into races in mid-season 'to confound the enemy' and some

Above: Built like a torpedo – the 2.5-liter Mercedes Grand Prix car.
Below: A stubbier later version with wind resistance lowered still further.
Below right: The 2.5-liter sports/racer, probably the loveliest streamlined shape of the three.

used only for the very high speed races at Avus and Tripoli.

In the light of the modern fuel crisis, it is interesting to note that in 1938 and 1939, the Mercedes Grand Prix cars averaged $2\frac{1}{2}$ to 3 miles to the gallon. It was not gasoline, but a mixture of alcohol, benzole, ether, acetone and lead, the precise formula being the secret of the racing department's own chemists.

There was no motor racing in Germany in 1946 although Daimler-Benz AG resumed car production; and it was not until 1950 that racing could be resumed.

The first 'new' Mercedes were hybrids. Neubauer found two of the 1939 3-liter racers at Unterturkheim and two more in a scrapyard in Berlin. From these four cars in varying states of repair, two serviceable models were put together with a third as training car.

Trials began with Lang, Caracciola and Karl Kling as drivers but Caracciola dropped out when the team manager revealed his plan to race in the Argentine in three month's time. Seeking a replacement, Neubauer went after and eventually secured a bandy-legged Argentinian who had shaken Europe by finishing second in the 1950 World Championship at the age of 39. His name was Juan Manuel Fangio. Mercedes finished second and third in both the Buenos Aires Grand Prix and the Evita Peron Grand Prix, the last race for the 3-liter cars.

It was obvious that if Mercedes were to resume their winning ways on the race circuits of the world, a new Grand Prix car would have to be built. There was a problem. Apart from the huge sum of money involved, the existing formula had only two years to run and it would take at least a year to design and build a new car.

Chief Designer Dr Nallinger and Head of Research, the famed Rudolf Uhlenhaut, came up with an idea. Why not forget about Grand Prix racing for the moment and concentrate on sportscar racing which was enjoying great popularity, not least in the United States? The basis of a suitable car already existed, the latest passenger car, the 300. Thus was born, in 1952, the first Mercedes sportscar for many a year, the 300SL (SL standing for Sport Light). The designation indicated that the original frame had been replaced by a light but very stiff lattice structure of thin welded tubing. The outer covering was also very light as the lattice structure had to bear all the stress. The engine, which was developed from that of Model 300S, was obliquely mounted to provide a better view head. Another innovation were upward opening gullwing doors, a constructive suggestion on solving the problem of getting in and out of low lying sportscars.

On 2 May 1952 Mercedes returned to European motor racing for the first time since 1939 in the classic Mille Miglia. There was trouble before the start when the Italians protested – no one knows why – against the gullwing doors. The German team had covered some 45,000 miles in practice but while the cars were new the drivers were old: Caracciola (51), Lang (43) and Kling (40). Lang crashed but Kling drove well to finish second after being in the lead much of the way. Caracciola, winner 21 years before, was fourth. Two weeks later he drove his last race, crashing in the Swiss GP which was run as a sportscar race.

Mercedes finished first, second and third but Caracciola, doomed to two years in a wheelchair, never raced again. He died in 1959, aged 58. He had won 100 international races, was four times European Champion, and was regarded by his team manager as the greatest driver who ever lived.

Air brakes were experimented with but it was decided not to risk them in the 24-Hour Race at Le Mans. Lang and Reiss

won anyway after a Frenchman, Pierre Levegh (otherwise Bouillon) driving solo, had led for 23 hours. Neubauer noted his name, a move which was later to have tragic consequences. Four Mercedes dominated the German Grand Prix with Lang again the winner and in November the team went to South America where in the 1945 mile Carrera Panamerica, Kling came first and Lang second.

The 300SL went into general production in 1954, truly a race-proven car, and many improvements were made as à result of the experience gained in racing. A striking feature of the engine was the use of direct fuel injection for each cylinder. This remarkable sportscar had a maximum speed of 166mph to which it could accelerate smoothly in top gear from 15mph.

The Mercedes backroom workers had not, however, been devoting all their time to sportscars. On 4 July 1954 Germany's footballers beat Hungary in the World Cup Final in Berne. On that day also the Mercedes Silver Arrows reappeared in a Grand Prix event for the first time in fifteen years.

Technically, the new car, the W196, was a great advance. It had an eight-cylinder engine at an angle of 60 degrees to make the front of the car flatter and less wind resistant. Its 2.5 liters produced 280bhp and a maximum speed of 187mph. It was the first Grand Prix car to have desmodromic valve gear, that is, mechanically and positively operated. Rolland-Pillain had experimented with this in 1922 and Duesenberg in 1931 but apart from Salmson, who used it in voiturette racing in 1926, no one seems to have persevered with it. The W196 was also the first Grand Prix car to have inboard shaft driven front brakes, a practice which was to be revived by Lotus in 1970. In a further bid to cut down wind resistance, a streamlined shell covered the front wheels.

When the new cars lined up for the French Grand Prix at Reims, Fangio, Kling and Hermann were the drivers. Hermann had to retire but Kling chased the Argentinian all the way and was just four yards behind when the checkered flag fell. It was a good start for the W196 but on Silverstone's airfield circuit the cars did not seem well-suited and the

Italian Ferraris were triumphant. For the European Grand Prix at the Nurburgring modifications were made including exposing the front wheels and Fangio duly won. Fangio also took the Swiss and Italian GPs to become 1954 World Champion.

On the other side of the world there was an echo of the early history of Daimler and Benz when Australian Stan Jones won the first New Zealand Grand Prix in a Maybach Special. Nearly thirty years later, his son Alan, would win the World Championship.

It was a busy and exciting time for Daimler-Benz AG. Back on top in Grand Prix racing, their winning sportscars were much in demand and their passenger cars were selling well. The 300SL was in general production, as already mentioned, and now came the racing sportscar, 300SLR, which in design and structure, owed much to the 2.5-liter racing car. A fellow 1955 debutant was the two-seat sports tourer, the

190SL, a 118mph, four-cylinder car, versatile enough for racing, touring or town driving.

The Racing Department still had Fangio under contract but Neubauer needed a strong young back up driver and so he signed England's Stirling Moss, Kling being the third driver. They were hardly needed. Fangio won in Argentina, Belgium, Holland and Italy although Moss won at Aintree and became the first Englishman to win the British Grand Prix. For the second time driving for Mercedes Fangio was World Champion. It gave the W196 a tremendous record: fifteen races entered in 1954 and 1955, twelve won, one taking the first four places, another when they took the first three and no less than seven where Mercedes finished first and second.

Further Mercedes' successes in sportscars were overshadowed by the tragedy of Le Mans when Levegh's car hurtled into the crowd and many were killed and injured in motor racing's worst ever disaster. The controversy over

exactly what happened has never died down but it is not the place to rake over the ashes here.

It might have been one of the great races of all time for the 300SLR Mercedes had worthy adversaries in the D-type Jaguars and 4.5-liter Ferraris. Apart from a string of great drivers – Fangio, Moss, Hawthorn, Castellotti and many more – there was much of technical interest in the cars.

The Mercedes were the first cars to race at Le Mans using fuel injection. Against this they were surprisingly not equipped with disk brakes, unlike the Jaguars. Feeling this put them at some disadvantage Mercedes decided to employ the air brake they had discarded the year before. This was the first time such a brake had been used in road racing. It took the form of an hydraulically operated arm the full width of the car panel, located behind the cockpit, which could be raised by the driver as required to supplement the old fashioned drum brakes. How much brakes were developing was demonstrated by the Triumph team, their cars being equipped with production type disks.

Ferrari had looked likely to win the Sports Car Championship that year, the first time it had been staged, but Jaguars took Le Mans and Moss won both the Mille Miglia (the only non Italian to do so apart from Caracciola) and the British Tourist Trophy to add to Fangio's victory in the Swedish Grand Prix, run that year as a sportscar race. To make sure of the title Mercedes had to change their plans and go to the Targa Florio which they had intended to miss. It was worthwhile going because Moss won again and the championship was Mercedes'.

Below: The 1955 version of the W196 Grand Prix racer. The W196 won twelve of the fifteen races in which it was entered in 1954 and 1955, filling the first four places in one and the first three in another. They were first and second in seven more races.

Hardly was the race over than Neubauer received a cable. The directors of Daimler-Benz AG had decided to withdraw from racing 'for several years.' It was a sad end to a season in which the team had earned two World Championships, the American Sports Car Championship (Paul O'Shea, 300SL) and the European Touring Car Championship (Werner Engel).

'Several years' have become many. Like many another manufacturer Daimler-Benz AG has obviously decided that today there is little to be learned from Grand Prix racing or even sports car racing, the cars in both categories having moved far from the normal passenger saloon or roadster. Most of Mercedes sporting achievements since 1955 have been in the realm of rallying.

In 1960, through their top drivers, Walter Shock and Rolf Moll, they took the rally championship. Eugen Bohringer, probably the greatest German rally driver of all, won the European Championship again for Mercedes in 1962 by taking the honors in the Acropolis, the Polish and the Liege-Sofia-Liege Rallies. The following year, driving the new 230SL he again won the Liege and the Acropolis fell to him in a 300SE.

The Mercedes cars of today, big and powerful, are not ideal for the majority of international rallies which tend to consist of comparatively short special stages, often on loose surfaces. Where Mercedes have distinguished themselves is in the long distance type of rally such as the World Cup and the London to Sydney Marathon. Typical was the 1980 season when the 450 was rallied. In the tough and rugged East African Safari, Mercedes were second (Mikkola and Hertz) and fourth (Cowan and Syer). In the Bandama Rally on the Ivory Coast in West Africa, the 450s filled the first three positions: Mikkola-Hertz, Waldegaard-Thorzelius and Cowan-Kaiser. In more conventional events, however, they did not enjoy the same degree of success.

Bjorn Waldegaard, the big Swede who won the first ever World Rally Drivers Championship in 1979 and joined the Mercedes works team the following year, commented: 'The Mercedes coupe is an extremely big car for rallies and you

have to accept that it is only suitable for certain events such as the Safari, Bandama and similar long distance rallies.'

Will Mercedes ever come back to top class motor racing? It can be assumed that if they do it will be with all the skill and ability, all the competence and professionalism which has always distinguished their ventures in to this field.

Meanwhile, from time to time come reminders of the great days that were. Among the entries for the 1982 RAC Golden Fifty Rally to celebrate 50 years of the RAC, were the names of Eugen Bohringer and Hermann Eger, 1962 European Rally Champions (there was no world championship then), driving a 1963 300SE. Every year in the Brighton Run, some of the great Mercedes of the pre 1905 era take part and if Gottlieb Daimler is looking down from above he must be proud that nearly 100 years after he himself took part in the event these cars are still running and still magnificent. Indeed, although the Run is not a race as many think, the Mercedes cannot resist opening up and one or other of them is often first across the line.

In the old Racing Department in Stuttgart there is still some activity. Three racers, two prewar and one postwar, are being rebuilt. The 1937 Type W125 is being rebuilt from the ground up including a reconditioned engine 'found on a shelf' according to former Technical Director Rudolf Uhlenhaut. The engine was stripped down, probably for the first time since 1938, and was found to be in excellent condition. Little work was required to 'make it as good as new.' The other prewar car was a 1939 Type W163 with which Hermann Lang won the European Championship (again there was no world title then). 'If it held together, Lang won the race,' commented Uhlenhaut, 'it was as simple as that.'

The third model to be renovated is the W196 2.5-liter straight eight which Mercedes raced in 1954.

All three are destined for the Stuttgart museum but as Mercedes showed when they visited Donington and Hermann Lang demonstrated one of the prewar cars they are not averse to airing their treasures so that some lucky enthusiasts may yet hear again the full throated roar of those powerful engines.

Two versions of the 300SLR sports racer. Below: One showing the driver-operated shield fitted in 1955 to aid braking and combat the disk brakes fitted to rivals.

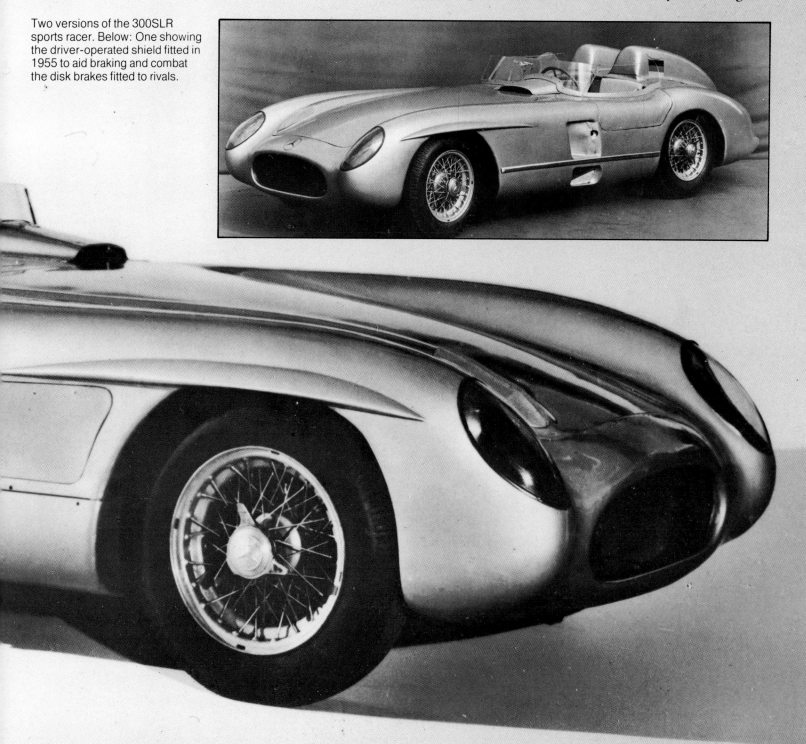

Above: The 1982 500SL – what more could a man ask? And how many people would be proud to be asked even to ride in such luxurious but dashing comfort?

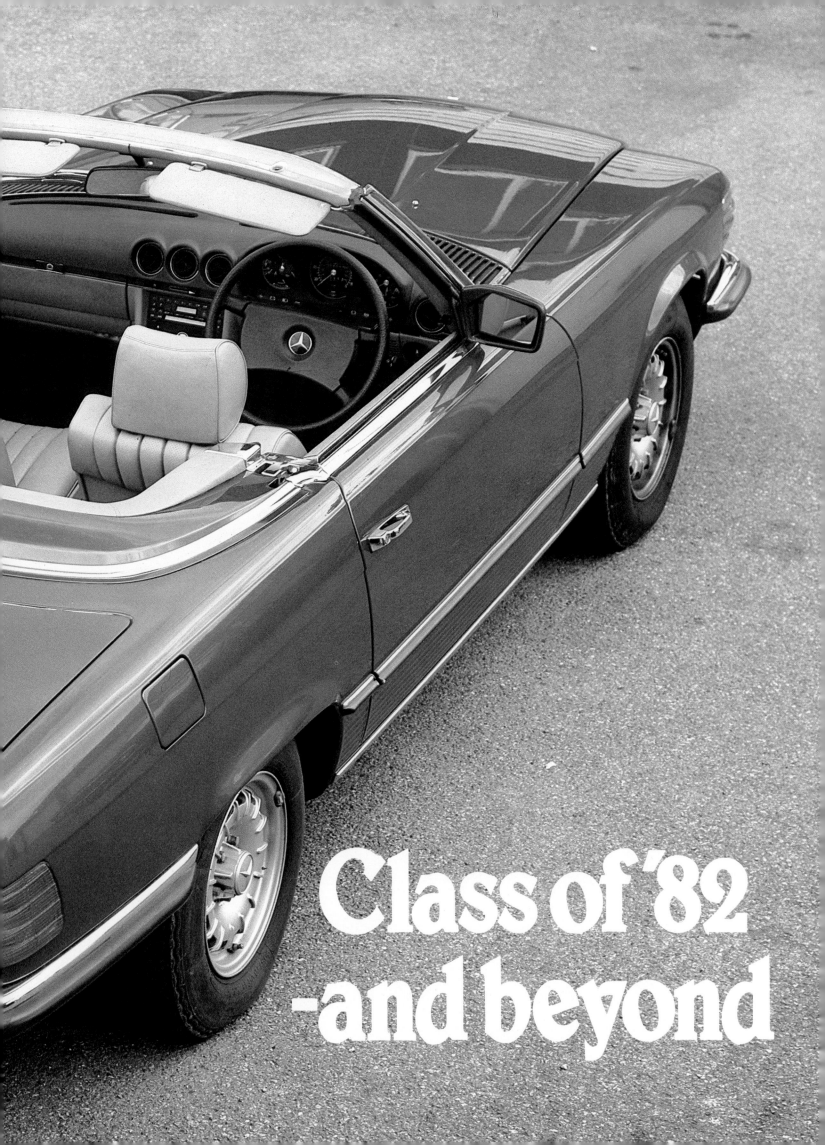

Class of '82
-and beyond

The Mercedes enthusiast who gazed into a showroom window and saw before his startled eyes an SS, an SS 29 and a 540K, might think himself a lucky man. When he took another look and realized that the cars were new, he would surely begin to wonder. The answer is that by 1982, at least three companies were marketing replicas labelled as Mercedes and others were producing cars which bore a strong resemblance to some of the Mercedes range, even if not bearing the name.

In Austria, the firm of Ledl offer in kit form, the 'Mercedes SS29', traditional open sports car, at 94,800 schillings. Sbarro, in Switzerland, produce an impressive replica, '1938 Mercedes-Benz 540K,' a roadster with a fiberglass body, at 200,000 Swiss francs. This car has a 5-liter engine with four-speed automatic transmission 'as used in today's 500SE.' In the United States, Moselle Speciality Cars market a '1928 Mercedes SS Roadster' designed by Jules Kaplan. Alas, for the enthusiast, Mr Kaplan's imagination has rather run away with him and although the honeycomb radiator looks familiar, the frame is a stretched version of the Ford Courier mini pickup chassis which would probably make Paul Daimler and Ferdinand Porsche wince. It has a standard Ford four-cylinder 2.3-liter engine and will cost the wife of the man who has everything else US $35,000 should she wish to buy him a birthday present.

The true enthusiast will be more than content with the present Mercedes range, the heartbeat of which is the New S and variants, a heartbeat which is still expected to be going strong in AD 2000, according to the company's top executives. Development of these cars started seven years before their 1980 launching and says Head of Development, Professor Werner Breitschwerdt, 'Few design teams in the world are given the chance to start again with virtually a fresh sheet of paper when they start to develop a new model.'

Fresh sheet or no, the Professor and his colleagues were well aware of several factors: Mercedes already made passenger cars which had a high reputation for comfort, performance and quality; that sales of the original S, which the New S was to replace, were increasing all the time; and that the average mileage covered by Mercedes owners was 16,000 miles per year (25,000km), about twice as much as the statistical average of all cars in Germany (the percentage of

Below: A car you cannot have enough of: the 500SL. Left: Detail of the instrument panel. Above left: The steering wheel. Above The de-luxe seating and interior. Also note the sun visors clipped to the windshield.

Above: The 1982 Diesel-engined 240TD Estate car. A powerful and versatile load-carrier, the Diesel also gives economical running.
Left: The rear door and the engine compartment.
Below right: The companion to the 240TD is the 1982 280E.

mileage driven in towns was appreciably lower and the percentage of miles driven on autobahns was much higher than average).

They were also well aware that the company expected them to produce a car which would have to meet requirements prevailing at any given time from the launching well into the 1990s. They would be expected to demonstrate how cars can be big and yet more fuel efficient and they would be expected to evolve higher standards of performance, comfort and safety.

Predictably, the New S was unmistakably Mercedes. Yet the familiar appearance disguised many improvements, some of which have already been described under the headings of energy and safety.

The type of forward looking effort which went into the New S is well demonstrated where seatbelts are concerned. For many years, critics have been saying that a major weakness of the seatbelt is that it is not adaptable to the varying heights of car occupants. It was left to Mercedes to do something about it by introducing, as mentioned earlier, the three position control adjustable for height.

Other features brought in included changing the front wheel suspension to improve running and handling, reducing engine and wind noise and improving lateral stability by increasing the length of the wheelbase.

A completely new electronically-controlled ventilation and heating system made it possible for the driver to adjust the temperature of the passenger compartment, including the backseat area. A system of heating and ventilation nozzles

not unlike those in passenger aircraft made for better passenger comfort and there was also a pressure extraction system for vitiated air through the luggage compartment.

A novel feature on those cars fitted with the optionally available electric seat adjustment was a seatshaped switch on the door. Moving the shape in the desired direction automatically moves the seat itself according to the occupant's wishes.

Another small detail, but one which will save motorists time and money in trips to the repair shop, was to be seen on the bumper units. These were foamclad with polyurethane and matched in appearance the protection strips along the sides. They gave way and absorbed minor shocks, regaining their shape afterwards.

On a similar theme, better access to major units for servicing purposes was developed and the service intervals themselves extended.

An optional extra on V8 models was hydropneumatic suspension.

But the areas in which the New S made the most spectacular progress was in aerodynamics and weight saving. The previous S had a good aerodynamic shape but the New S achieved the remarkably low drag factor of 0.36.

Thus, at the time of writing the complete Mercedes range encompasses the following:

200: a four door saloon with four-cylinder gasoline engine.

200D: the same car, this time with a Diesel engine.

200T: for use as an estate car with an additional door at the rear.

230E: a four door saloon with four-cylinder gasoline engine.

230CE: the most expensive of this series, being a two door coupé.

230T: the 'estate' version.

250: four door saloon with six-cylinder gasoline engine.

250 Long Wheelbase: if you pay more you get a longer version.

250T: the rear door again.

240D: saloon with four-cylinder Diesel engine.

240D Long Wheelbase: same car, longer wheelbase.

240TD: the 'estate' version but still with Diesel engine.

300D: saloon with five-cylinder Diesel.

300D Long Wheelbase: same car but longer.

300TD: the 'estate' version.

300TD Turbodiesel: same car with turbocharged engine.

280E: four door saloon with six-cylinder gasoline engine.

280CE: two door coupe version.

280TE: 'estate' version.

280S

280SE

280SEL

380SE   a total of seven four door saloons, the basic

380SEL   variations being engine power.

500SE

500SEL

380SEC: V8 coupe with a top speed of 130mph (210kph).

500SEC: similar car with a top speed of 140mph (226kph).

280SL: two door roadster with six-cylinder engine. Top speed is 121mph (195kph).

380SL: similar car with V8 engine and top speed 127mph (205kph).

500SL: V8 with top speed of 137mph (220kph).

230G: Mercedes utility vehicle, available as two door open, 2+1 station wagon and 4+1 long wheelbase station wagon.

280G: similar series with six-cylinder engines.

250GD: similar with four-cylinder Diesels.

300GD: similar with five-cylinder Diesels.

Thus a comprehensive range which only notably lacks a small town runabout.

However, Daimler-Benz engineers and designers are not content to rest on the laurels of the New S cars. A research car, the C111, provided the inspiration for many of the features now incorporated as standard in present day Mercedes and now there are new research cars bearing the name AUTO 2000. The prototype was unveiled in Frankfurt in September 1981.

Four years previously the German Federal Ministry for Research and Technology challenged the German motor industry to develop forward looking prototypes with a view towards maintaining the country's lead in automotive tech-

Below and left: The international fame achieved by the Jeep and the Land Rover has tended to obscure the fact that other highly efficient four-wheel drive cross-country utility vehicles are built elsewhere, notably this 1982 Mercedes 280GE.

nology on a longer term basis. The guidelines called for a 30 percent reduction in fuel consumption and accident-repair costs together with substantial reductions in noise and other emissions.

Taking the New S as their basic vehicle, the Mercedes scientists produced a windcheating body design containing a host of innovative ideas.

The New S represented an improvement of 14 percent in aerodynamic terms over its predecessors; Auto 2000 represented a further improvement of 20 percent.

Although derived from the de luxe saloons of the New S series, Auto 2000 has a body 201 inches (510cm) long and 72 inches (182cm) wide. This modification and others gave it a 0.30 drag coefficient with a body weight of 3528lb (1600kg).

And despite being a four-door saloon, the car has the rear-ward sloping radiator grill of the 380 and 500SEC coupes.

At the rear, the roofline was continued in the form of a transparent cover to the luggage space. The roofline was lowered and considerable improvement made to the airflow through the addition of underfloor panels and spoilers. A more controversial innovation is the use of fixed side windows with only a small openable panel for communication at car park entrances and exits, tolls and so forth.

Three different power units were made available, all of them allowing top speeds in the region of 124mph (200kph). Prototype No 1 had the most original power unit – a Diesel fed gas turbine engine capable of operating at an extremely high temperature and so well situated to compete with conventional gasoline and Diesel engines in terms of fuel consumption. Prototype No 2 was equipped with a light alloy 3.3-liter V6 turbocharged Diesel, two 150hp turbo-

Modern Mercs, a selection of 1982 models including (above right) 450SLC, (right) 300SEL and (below) 300D.
Far right: The Diesel-engined 300D growling, a symbol of the strength behind the proud name of Mercedes-Benz.

compressors being used. The third power unit is a 3.8-liter eight-cylinder gasoline engine.

To get the best out of the car, whatever the power unit fitted, a 'thinking' gearbox was invented, one which enables a driver who is prepared to forgo some of the engine's output in favor of reduced fuel consumption to drive more efficiently. In order to achieve this the automatic gearbox has three 'Drive' positions instead of the usual one.

The first of these positions is *economy*. This limits the engine output and the top speed by means of overriding the injection pump and gearbox. The second position is *city*. This provides low gearshift speeds in order to reduce fuel consumption and emissions when driving in congested city and town conditions. The third position is *fast*, which means that the driver can make optimum use of the engine's full output.

The automatic transmission is electrically and hydraulically controlled so that in each drive position the most fuel efficient gear is always selected, something that can be done mechanically far better than the average driver can do it manually. Road tests with the Diesel engine have given a consumption of 5.5 liters per 100km at 90kph.

There are many other exciting aspects of Auto 2000. As well as the already familiar antilock braking system, the car has a new device called an acceleration slip control. This regulates tire to road friction and cuts down on wasteful driving.

Sophisticated driver information, route planning and communication systems are also incorporated in the car and perhaps the most significant advance of all is collision avoidance radar which may well do in the future for the motorist what it has done for the seaman and pilot.

In its silver-and-black livery, Auto 2000 is already a very attractive car which, if it were on the world market, would undoubtedly enjoy considerable sales. By the year 2000 it may well be a vastly different car because it will be used to test every new idea which comes along and those which prove worthwhile will be incorporated in it. The Frankfurt Motor Show of AD 2000 should be well worth attending.

Meanwhile, Mercedes will continue to manufacture a quality product. After all, Jonathan Hart, of 'Hart to Hart', the only American TV series 'millionaire' who appears to be clean living and honest (would you buy a secondhand car from JR of 'Dallas' or Blake Carrington of 'Dynasty'?) drives a Mercedes roadster.

Appendix

1900/01   First Mercedes car
35hp 4 cylinder
Note Fitted with gate change 4-speed gearbox; first engine to have mechanically operated inlet valves
1902/03   Mercedes tourer
8/11hp 4 cylinder
12/16hp 4 cylinder
1902/06   Mercedes Simplex
18/22hp 4 cylinder
28/32hp 4 cylinder
40/45hp 4 cylinder
Note This became the world's leading car in the class not exceeding 1000kg (2200lb). It was appreciably lighter than the 35hp cars of 1900/01 and had a wheelbase of 2450mm and a track of 1450mm
60/70hp 4 cylinder
1903/04   Mercedes Simplex racing car
60hp 4 cylinder
90hp 4 cylinder
Note The name 'Simplex' was dropped after this
1904/05   Mercedes racing car
80hp 4 cylinder
100hp 4 cylinder
1905   Mercedes tourer
26/45hp 4 cylinder
31/55hp 4 cylinder
36/65hp 4 cylinder
1906   Mercedes tourer
37/70hp 6 cylinder
1906   Mercedes racing car
120hp 6 cylinder
1907   Mercedes tourer
39/80hp 6 cylinder
1908   Grand Prix racing car
135hp 4 cylinder

1908/13   Mercedes shaf-driven car
8/18hp 4 cylinder
10/20hp 4 cylinder
14/35hp 4 cylinder
21/35hp 4 cylinder
22/40hp 4 cylinder
28/60hp 4 cylinder
Note These had poppet valve engines
1910/13   Mercedes Knight car
10/30hp 4 cylinder
16/40hp 4 cylinder
16/45hp 4 cylinder
25/65hp 4 cylinder
Note These had sleeve valve engines
1910/13   Mercedes chain-driven car
22/50hp 4 cylinder
28/60hp 4 cylinder
38/80hp 4 cylinder
37/90hp 4 cylinder
Note These had poppet valve engines
1914   Mercedes tourer
28/95hp 6 cylinder
1914   Grand Prix racing car
115hp 4 cylinder
1916   Mercedes Knight car
16/50hp 4 cylinder
1919   Tourer
10/35hp 4 cylinder 2.6 liter
1921/22   Production car
with supercharger
6/25/40hp 4 cylinder 1.5 liter
10/40/65hp 4 cylinder 2.6 liter
1924   Racing car with supercharger
120hp 4 cylinder 2.0 liter
1924   Racing car with supercharger
160hp 8 cylinder 2.0 liter
1924   Tourer with supercharger
15/70(100hp 6 cylinder 4.0 liter
24/100/140hp 6 cylinder 6.0 liter

Amalgamation with Benz

1926   Stuttgart 200
8/38hp 6 cylinder 2.0 liter
1926   Mannheim
12/55hp 6 cylinder 3.1 liter
1926   Sports car K (super)
24/110/160 6 cylinder 6.25 liter
1927   Mannheim 300
12/55hp 6 cylinder 3.2 liter
1927   Sports car S (super)
26/120/185 6 cylinder 6.8 liter
1928   Stuttgart 260
10/50hp 6 cylinder 2.6 liter
1928   Mannheim 350
14/70hp 6 cylinder 3.5 liter
1928   Nurburg 460   y
18/80hp 8 cylinder 4.6 liter
1928   Sports car SS (super)
27/140/200 6 cylinder 7.1 liter
1928   Sportscar SSK (super)
27/170/225 6 cylinder 7.1 liter
1929   Mannheim 370
15/75hp 6 cylinder 3.7 liter
1930   Super Mercedes with or without super
30/150/200 8 cylinder 7.7 liter
Note Rigid axles
1931   170
7/32hp 6 cylinder 1.7 liter
Note First swing axle type
1931   Mannheim 370K (short) 370S (sports)
15/75hp 6 cylinder 3.7 liter
1931   Nurburg 500
19/110hp 8 cylinder 4.9 liter
1931   Racing sports car SSKL with supercharger
27/170/300 6 cylinder 7.1 liter
1932   200 (short and long)
8/40hp 6 cylinder 2 liter
1933   290
11/68hp 6 cylinder 2.9 liter
1933   Sports convertible 380 with supercharger
15/90/140 8 cylinder 3.8 liter
1933   130
26hp 4 cylinder 1.3 liter
Note First rear-mounted engine
1934   Sports car 150H
55hp 4 cylinder 1.5 liter

1934   Sports car 500K (super)
100/160hp 8 cylinder 5 liter
1934   Formula racing car 750kg
354hp 8 cylinder 3.36 liter
1934   Record breaking car
398hp 8 cylinder 3.71 liter
1935   170H
38hp 4 cylinder 1.7 liter
1935   17 &V
38hp 4 cylinder 1.7 liter
1935   260D
45hp 4 cylinder 2.6 liter
Note First Diesel passenger car
1935   Formula racing car 750kg
430hp 8 cylinder 3.99 liter
1935   Formula racing car 750kg
462hp 8 cylinder 4.31 liter
1936   230 (box type frame)
55hp 6 cylinder 2.3 liter
1936   Sports convertible 540K with supercharger
115/180hp 8 cylinder 5.4 liter
1936   Formula racing car 750kg with compressor
494hp 8 cylinder 4.14 liter
1936   Record-breaking car
540hp V12 cylinder 4.98 liter
1937   320
78hp 6 cylinder 3.2 liter
1937   Sports car
50hp 4 cylinder 2.0 liter
1937   Formula racing car 750kg with compressor
646hp 8 cylinder 5.66 liter
1938   Super Mercedes (super)
155/230hp 8 cylinder 7.7 liter
Note Swing axles
1938   230 (x-frame)
55hp 6 cylinder 2.3 liter
1938   320
78hp 6 cylinder 3.4 liter
1938   Record breaking car
736hp V12 cylinder 5.57 liter
1939   Record breaking car
476hp V12 cylinder 3.0 liter
1939   Racing car (2-stage super)
254hp V8 cylinder 1.5 liter
1939   Formula racing car (2-stage)
483hp V12 cylinder 3.0 liter
1946   17 &V (resumed)
38hp 4 cylinder 1.7 liter

1949   170S
52hp 4 cylinder 1.7 liter
1949   170D
38hp 4 cylinder 1.7 liter
1950   17 &Va
45hp 4 cylinder 1.8 liter
1950   170Da
40hp 4 cylinder 1.8 liter
1951   220
80hp 6 cylinder 2.2 liter
1951   300
115hp 6 cylinder 3.0 liter
1952   300S
150hp 6 cylinder 3.0 liter
1952   300SL carburetor
175hp 6 cylinder 3.0 liter
1952   170Vb
45hp 4 cylinder 1.8 liter
1952   170Sb
40hp 4 cylinder 1.8 liter
1952   170Db and Ds
52hp 4 cylinder 1.8 liter
1953   1705-V
45hp 4 cylinder 1.8 liter
1953   170S-D
40hp 4 cylinder 1.8 liter
1953   180 (side valve motor)
52hp 4 cylinder 1.8 liter
1953   180D
40hp 4 cylinder 1.8 liter
Note 43hp as of 1955
1954   220 coupe
85hp 6 cylinder 2.2 liter
1954   220a
85hp 6 cylinder 2.2 liter
1954   300b
125hp 6 cylinder 3.0 liter
1954, 300SL petrol injection
215hp 6 cylinder 3.0 liter
1954   Formula racing car
280hp 8 cylinder 2.5 liter
1955   300SLR racing sports car
300hp 8 cylinder 3.0 liter
1955   190SL sports car
105hp 4 cylinder 1.9 liter
1955   300c/300c automatic
125hp 6 cylinder 3.0 liter
1955   300Sc petrol injection
175hp 6 cylinder 3.0 liter
1956   190
75hp 4 cylinder 1.9 liter

1956   219
85hp 6 cylinder 2.2 liter
Note 90hp as of 1957
1956   220S
100hp 6 cylinder 2.2 liter
Note 106hp as of 1957
1957   180a, motor with ohc
65hp 4 cylinder 1.89 liter
1957   300d automatic
160hp 6 cylinder 3.0 liter
1957   300SL roadster, p.i.
215hp 6 cylinder 3.0 liter
1958   190D
50hp 4 cylinder 1.9 liter
1958   220SE, p.i.
115hp 6 cylinder 2.2 liter
1959   180b
68hp 4 cylinder 1.8 liter
1959   180Db
43hp 4 cylinder 1.8 liter
1959   190b
80hp 4 cylinder 1.9 liter
1959   190Db
50hp 4 cylinder 1.9 liter
1959   220b
95hp 6 cylinder 2.2 liter
1959   220Sb
110hp 6 cylinder 2.2 liter
1959   220SEb, p.i.
120hp 6 cylinder 2.2 liter
1961   180c
68hp 4 cylinder 1.89 liter
1961   180Dc
48hp 4 cylinder 1.99 liter
1961   190c
80hp 4 cylinder 1.9 liter
1961   190Dc
55hp 4 cylinder 1.99 liter
1961   220SE/c, p.i.
120hp 6 cylinder 2.2 liter
1961   300SE, p.i.
160hp 6 cylinder 3.0 liter
Note 170hp as of 1964
1963   230SL, p.i.
150hp 6 cylinder 2.3 liter
1963   600 Super Mercedes, p.i.
250hp V8 cylinder 6.3 liter
1965   200
95hp 4 cylinder 2.0 liter
1965   200D
55hp 4 cylinder 2.0 liter

1965   230
105hp 6 cylinder 2.3 liter
1965   230S
120hp 6 cylinder 2.3 liter
1965   250S
130hp 6 cylinder 2.5 liter
1965   250SE, p.i.
150hp 6 cylinder 2.5 liter
1965   300SEb, p.i.
170hp 6 cylinder 3.0 liter
1965   300SEL, p.i.
170hp 6 cylinder 3.0 liter
1967   250SL
150hp 6 cylinder 2.5 liter
1968   200D
55hp 4 cylinder 2.0 liter
1968   220D
60hp 4 cylinder 2.2 liter
1968   200
95hp 4 cylinder 2.0 liter
1968   220
105hp 4 cylinder 2.2 liter
1968   230
120hp 6 cylinder 2.3 liter
1968   250
130hp 6 cylinder 2.5 liter
1968   280S
140hp 6 cylinder 2.8 liter
1968   280SE, p.i.
160hp 6 cylinder 2.8 liter
1968   280SE, p.i., convertible
and coupe
160hp 6 cylinder 2.8 liter
1968   280SL, p.i.
170hp 6 cylinder 2.8 liter
1968   300SEL, p.i.
250hp V8 cylinder 6.3 liter
1968   250C coupe
130hp 6 cylinder 2.5 liter
1968   250CE coupe, p.i.
150hp 6 cylinder 2.5 liter
1968   280SEL, p.i.
170hp 6 cylinder 2.8 liter
1969   280SE, p.i., convertible
and coupe
200hp V8 cylinder 3.5 liter
1969   300SEL, p.i.
200hp V8 cylinder 3.5 liter
1970   280SE/SEL, p.i.
200hp V8 cylinder 3.5 liter
1971   350SL, p.i.
200hp V8 cylinder 3.5 liter
1971   350SLC coupe, p.i.
200hp V8 cylinder 3.5 liter
1972   280
160hp 6 cylinder 2.8 liter
1972   280E, p.i.
185hp 6 cylinder 2.8 liter
1972   280C coupe
160hp 6 cylinder 2.8 liter
1972   280CE coupe, p.i.
185hp 6 cylinder 2.8 liter

1972   280S
160hp 6 cylinder 2.8 liter
1972   280SE, p.i.
185hp 6 cylinder 2.8 liter
1972   350SE, p.i.
200hp V8 cylinder 3.5 liter
1976   W123 200
94hp 4 cylinder 2.0 liter
1976   W123 200D
4 cylinder 2.0 liter
1976   W123 240D
4 cylinder 2.4 liter
1976   W123 230
109hp 4 cylinder 2.3 liter
1976   W123 300D
80hp 5 cylinder 3.0 liter
1976   W123 250
129hp 6 cylinder 2.5 liter
1976   W123 280E
185hp 6 cylinder 2.8 liter
1977   230C coupe
109hp 4 cylinder 2.3 liter
1977   280CE coupe
185hp 6 cylinder 2.8 liter
1979   240YD estate
4 cylinder 2.4 liter
1979   300TD estate
5 cylinder 3.0 liter
1979   250T estate
6 cylinder 2.5 liter
1979   280TE estate
6 cylinder 2.8 liter
1980   S Class 280SE
185hp 6 cylinder
1980   S Class 380SE
218hp V8 cylinder
1980   S Class 500SE
240hp V8 cylinder
1980   380SL two-seater
118hp V8 cylinder 3.8 liter
1980   380SLC fixed head coupe
118hp V8 cylinder 3.8 liter
1980   500SL two-seater
240hp V8 cylinder 5.0 liter
Note Also in 1980 new, more powerful
engines (4 cylinder) for 200 (109hp)
and 230 (136hp), now designated
230E for injection and same engine
fitted in 230CE coupe and 230CE
estate car. 200T estate car with
estate car. 200T estate car with
uprated 2 liter engine
1981   380SEC fixed head coupe
118hp V8 cylinder 3.8 liter
1981   500SEC fixed head coupe
240hp V8 cylinder 5.0 liter
Note Also 'Energy Concept' introduced
with a number of modifications
designed to reduce fuel consumption
right across the board (see text)
Different Specifications apply in some
cases to USA. Thus 300CD (coupe
Diesel), 300 SD (S Class with turbo
Diesel, etc).

Index

Acknowledgments

The author and the publishers would like to thank Nick Georgano, Bridget Daly and Richard Nichols for their help in editing the book, David Eldred who designed it and Ronald Watson who compiled the index.

Special credit is due to Nicky Wright who took most of the photographs and to Mercedes-Benz for supplying archive material.

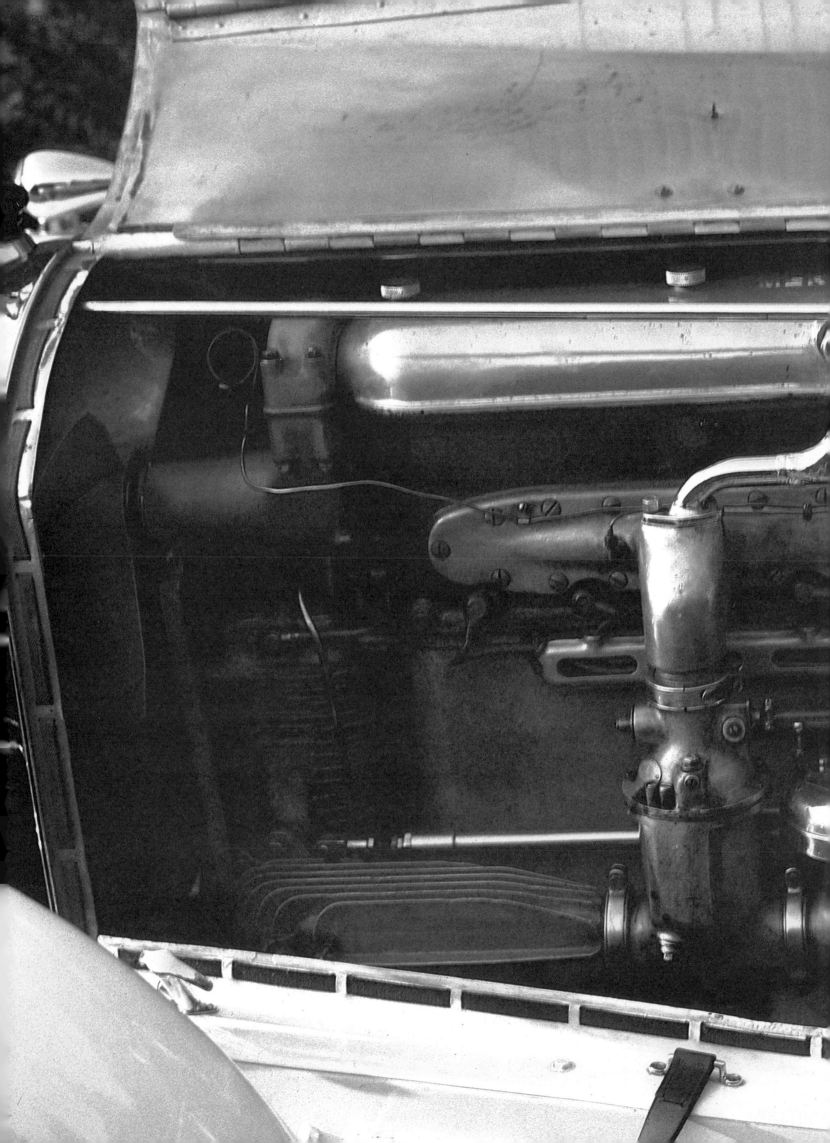